The Emerging Work of Today's Superintendent

PRAISE FOR *THE EMERGING WORK OF TODAY'S SUPERINTENDENT*

"Leading school districts to be successful for all students requires new thinking that expands beyond the boundaries of what was traditionally called school. Philip D. Lanoue and Sally J. Zepeda describe a changing educational and community landscape that requires new questions to be asked by superintendents and school leaders. *The Emerging Work of Today's Superintendent: Leading Schools and Communities to Educate All Children* creates a context for leader reflection as today's educational system is redesigned to educate *all* children to reach their full potential."

—**Robert Avossa**, EdD, superintendent, the School District of Palm Beach County, West Palm Beach, Florida

"An excellent, thoughtful read for new and veteran superintendents, as they seek to embrace the leadership role necessary for the rapid fire changes taking place in the world of K–12 education. The authors encourage boldness in vision, mission, and goals, and call for an agreed focus on learning between the board and superintendent. Calculated risk taking on behalf of student success is not only suggested but encouraged. They clearly get the necessity for trust, collaboration, and innovation at all levels. Importantly, this book supports system transformation by shining a spotlight on the danger of allowing adult issues to derail the focus on student success."

—**Valarie Wilson**, executive director, the Georgia School Boards Association

The Emerging Work of Today's Superintendent

Leading Schools and Communities to Educate All Children

Philip D. Lanoue and Sally J. Zepeda

PUBLISHED IN PARTNERSHIP WITH
THE SCHOOL SUPERINTENDENTS ASSOCIATION

ROWMAN & LITTLEFIELD
Lanham • Boulder • New York • London

Published in partnership with The School Superintendents Association

Published by Rowman & Littlefield
A wholly owned subsidiary of The Rowman & Littlefield Publishing Group, Inc.
4501 Forbes Boulevard, Suite 200, Lanham, Maryland 20706
www.rowman.com

Unit A, Whitacre Mews, 26-34 Stannary Street, London SE11 4AB

British Library Cataloguing in Publication Information Available

Library of Congress Cataloging-in-Publication Data Is Available

ISBN: 978-1-4758-3550-2 (cloth : alk. paper)
ISBN: 978-1-4758-3551-9 (paper : alk. paper)
ISBN: 978-1-4758-3552-6 (electronic)

♾™ The paper used in this publication meets the minimum requirements of American National Standard for Information Sciences—Permanence of Paper for Printed Library Materials, ANSI/NISO Z39.48-1992.

Printed in the United States of America

Contents

Preface

In this book, *The Emerging Work of Today's Superintendent: Leading Schools and Communities to Educate All Children*, we present a great deal about the "thinking" processes that can support superintendents as they lead their systems. This book is not designed to be a "traditional how-to book" with prescriptive steps for superintendents to follow.

This book focuses on the changing role of the superintendent who now must lead with new skills in a time when the landscape of communities is shifting, necessitating the mobilization of people through advocacy and activism alongside new partnerships with businesses, local governmental agencies, and community organizations.

To lead districts, superintendents must ask new questions about current school structures while navigating changes in local, state, and federal education policies to ensure practices are aligned to meet the needs of all children. Key questions throughout the book help leaders to create coherence in a system of change while leading the learning for members in the district and developing effective governance structures to empower leaders in making strategic decisions.

Superintendents must focus efforts on leading systems to think through the world of information and digital access, so students can learn for tomorrow and to leverage social media to brand and support system-wide transformations. The frenetic work, roles, and responsibilities of the superintendent requires personal and professional balance to be effective in leading districts and communities.

While many elements of what superintendents must do have remained constant, we present a foray of questions to spark new thinking about the work, roles, and responsibilities of the superintendent. Our overall goal in writing this book was to engage superintendents and leaders by asking different questions about their roles in leading schools and communities. These questions are critically important because system leaders need to engage in new conversations that lead adults to make the changes and to accept the responsibility for educating all children. Given this goal and its rationale, the purposes of this book are to:

1. Help leaders to think through what's needed to lead new systems.
2. Develop and lead collaborative structures within the district and their communities.
3. Identify changing leadership approaches, the broad set of responsibilities, and inclusive processes that support opportunities for all students to succeed.

Our belief is that adhering to the current thinking found in too many districts will not move schools or help all children learn what they need to be successful in their world. Leading schools for tomorrow involves commitments to a new vision that is aligned to strategic planning and leading communities.

Superintendents who can mobilize people and systems are adept at developing new partnerships with businesses, local government, and support organizations because schools cannot do this work alone. Tomorrow will be very different than today, and because of the inability to predict tomorrow based on today, superintendents must embrace the potential of the digital space, taking calculated risks on behalf of students and their access to information. Superintendents are architects of change and must be able to engage in effective decision-making through governance structures including the local board of education.

Today's superintendents and leaders must find one voice to engage in advocacy for their systems. This book provides new concepts for superintendents to reflect on current leader practices within and outside of the system.

Acknowledgments

Writing a book and pushing the send button to the publisher are two different things. Many people worked behind the scenes to make this work possible. We take this opportunity to thank Phillip D. Grant and Sevda Yildirim, both PhD students in Educational Administration and Policy at the University of Georgia, for their support with behind the scenes work. They always found time to chase references, support the development of the index, and a host of other tasks associated with meeting our deadlines.

We thank the external reviewers who gave us feedback on the initial proposal. The guidance helped us to make sound decisions as we framed our writing.

We are indebted to the talented teachers and leaders who have challenged us in our thinking, who have shared practices with us, and who have taught us lessons along the way. We hope that this book reflects the best thinking about the ways superintendents must now begin thinking about the leadership needed to lead districts in educating all children.

We were fortunate to have seven national leaders who agreed to share their perspectives about the work needed to keep the system balanced. The professionals whose perspectives are a part of chapter 8 include:

- Dr. Peter I. Burrows, superintendent of the Addison Central School District (Middlebury, Vermont)
- Mr. Dennis W. Dearden, president and cofounder of Monkey Business Associates (Oro Valley, Arizona)
- Dr. Susan Enfield, superintendent of the Highline Public Schools (Burien, Washington)
- Dr. Sybil Knight-Burney, superintendent of the Harrisburg School District (Harrisburg, Pennsylvania)

- Dr. Patrice Pujol, president of the National Institute for Excellence in Teaching (Baton Rouge, Louisiana)
- Dr. Grant Rivera, superintendent of the Marietta City Schools (Marietta, Georgia)
- Dr. Thomas S. Woods-Tucker, superintendent of Princeton City Schools (Cincinnati, Ohio)

Our book is stronger because of the insights and the wisdom shared by these professionals about being an executive leader.

We would be remiss if we did not acknowledge Dr. Thomas Koerner, vice president and publisher for education issues at Rowman & Littlefield for his absolute belief in this project. Tom's good-will and support were apparent from the start to the finish of this book. Thank you, Tom! We are likewise appreciative of Ms. Carlie Wall, managing editor at Rowman & Littlefield, who quickly responded to any questions we had along the way. Rounding out the team were Emily Eastridge, editorial assistant; Lisa Whittington, production editor; and others who worked behind the scenes to render a book we can take pride.

Finally, we thank the American Association of School Administrators (AASA) and James Minichello, Director of Communications and Marketing, for their readiness to endorse this work in supporting school superintendents. We are, indeed, humbled.

Introduction

Every chapter begins with a letter from a superintendent, followed by the topics for leaders, and then an introduction to amplify and organize the key areas of the chapter. We structured the book chapters in a way for the reader to look topically across the scope of responsibilities for superintendents to create learning environments where all students can grow and develop.

Each section of the chapters includes a space for the reader to pause with questions, bundled in sections titled *Reflecting on the Work*. At the end of each chapter, sections titled *A Superintendent's Dive* delve into the topics that encourage the reader to more fully understand the content as they assess their district's work and identify focus areas for their future consideration. Each chapter includes a list of suggested readings germane to the topics examined as well as references.

OVERVIEW OF THE CHAPTERS

Chapter 1: In *Leading in a New Landscape*, an overview broadly frames the new thinking for leaders in their efforts to redesign schools and programs that meet the individual needs of students. Superintendents need to examine their beliefs about the architecture of school, school cultures, the role of the community, and exercising their voices in advocating for all students.

Chapter 2: In *Coherence in a System of Change*, processes are outlined for superintendents to align the system with its vision, mission, and beliefs while developing a framework for school improvement planning. Superintendents must be able to establish coherence throughout the system through effective planning, timely monitoring, and making midcourse changes.

Chapter 3: In *Leading in Shifting Landscapes*, new ways of thinking are examined to leverage and maximize the assets of schools and their communities as students travel on a new education continuum. Superintendents must realize that the work in schools cannot be done without understanding the needs of shifting communities, which require districts to create new collaborative partnerships in educating all children.

Chapter 4: In *Leading the Learning*, new actions needed by superintendents are discussed to develop leadership within the work of the school board, principals, teachers, parents, and members in the community. Superintendents must be in roles where they serve as models for being current in the field, establishing collective leadership, and their ability to prepare leaders across and beyond the system.

Chapter 5: In *Leading in a World of Access*, the challenges and risks in designing programs that support new learning outcomes are described in a way that illustrates that students can be lifelong learners through internet access. Superintendents will need to create a new learner profile where students are able to innovate, communicate, collaborate, and synthesize information to be ready for jobs that do not exist today.

Chapter 6: In *The Voice of the Superintendent,* the role of the superintendent is outlined to promote activism in their advocacy for children and in creating a new vision using social media for communicating and branding the organization. Superintendents have a critical voice in moving the agenda for education from the schoolhouse to the policies at the state and federal levels using multiple communication avenues.

Chapter 7: In *The Dynamics of Governance,* effective governance models are examined to help schools and districts stay focused without being influenced by the distractions from external voices that often derail new work. Superintendents have a paramount role in establishing governance systems where roles are clearly defined and understand creating a common voice that ripples through the system.

Chapter 8: In *Your Balance Is the System's Balance,* insight from sitting and former superintendents provide perspective on balancing their lives knowing they are in the spotlight 24-7; needing time with their families given the enormity of the workload; and navigating their own philosophy with those of their communities. Superintendents' life balance is necessary for health in their personal and professional life and how they navigate the many decisions made every day.

Chapter 9: In *We Are All Responsible*, common themes throughout the book are identified, which illustrate ways for superintendents to refocus their work and to ensure coherence. For superintendents, the ultimate responsibility for educating all children is a simple answer to a very complex question; "we all do," when they see our emerging roles as school and community leaders.

Chapter 1

Leading in a New Landscape

IN THIS CHAPTER . . .

- New Beliefs
- Culture of Change
- Beliefs to Practices
- Shifting Communities
- Developing Leaders
- Digital Landscape
- Your Voice
- Decisions
- Social Media
- Balance

LETTER FROM THE SUPERINTENDENT

Dear Mrs. Thompson:

I enjoyed visiting your third-grade classroom yesterday. I was pleased to see the level of engagement by your students and the deliberate use of our instructional framework in your lesson design to teach our performance standards. I especially enjoyed your introduction of me to your class and their interesting responses. While many students know me and some of what I do, I am always intrigued by their perspectives. However, the responses by your students today caused me to think about my role and responsibilities as the district's leader. I believe my work is substantively different from those of past expectations. When students responded by asking, "Do you own the schools?" and, "What do you do?" I realized that these questions might be at the heart of it all in defining the new role of superintendents.

Thank you, Mrs. Thompson, for your commitment in challenging and caring for our children and for the opportunity for me to listen to our student's voices—it has made this experienced leader think and reflect on my work as we move to educate all children!

Sincerely,

Superintendent

The work of the superintendent to create a culture where all students thrive and achieve can no longer be an aspiration. A culture for student success must be a requirement that is not negotiable. Making student achievement the primary responsibility for superintendents will require significant changes in their roles and responsibilities as well as in their relationships with school boards, teachers, school leaders, parents, members of the community, and local and state government officials. Inevitably, superintendents will need to look within themselves to reflect on their beliefs about their roles with an openness to new directions. Schools will only transform when leaders assume very different approaches to their duties and responsibilities.

The transition into a new role is difficult given the complexities of education and the significance of all students in our society being successful. Today, we banner the outcome that all students can be successful; however, are districts and communities prepared to do what is necessary for this to happen? The most significant shift in creating an educational system that works for all students recognizes that student success is a collective adult responsibility and not a student problem.

The conversations about student success must be different, the adult participation must be different, and program designs must be different if we want different outcomes. As we engage with the reader throughout this book, we focus on the beliefs and actions of superintendents and the leadership required to initiate and sustain meaningful transformation in schools and their districts. Leading school transformation cannot occur in isolation and requires the mobilization of schools and their communities to embrace new approaches to the collective work required today.

NEW BELIEFS

Leading for schools that engage all students will require superintendents to reflect on their beliefs about educational design as well as their current responsibilities as educational leaders. Couros (2014) spoke to the primacy of change and beliefs, sharing,

As society continues to change, schools need to adapt to best serve our students for their future as well as their present. Those that are willing to adapt and learn from change now, will be the ones that are most likely to be successful in the future. (para. 3)

If schools are going to embrace the changes required for the future success of all students, then superintendents will need to ask new questions based on different beliefs about school design and outcomes. Leaders who hold strong convictions about the need to do the work differently will be those that make the most significant impact on student success.

Transforming schools can no longer be about leadership that maintains schools that meet the needs of some students for yesterday. Superintendents have a new responsibility in engaging themselves and members of their organization in continuous conversations about their beliefs and actions. Hirsh, Psencik, and Brown (2014) share, "Regularly discussing beliefs and assumptions opens up deeper understanding of ourselves and our colleagues" (p. 14). Superintendents have a significant impact on the organization when their beliefs and the beliefs of the organization are aligned. All students will be able to realize their success when superintendents take different actions based on new beliefs about school transformation.

CULTURE OF CHANGE

In the perennial era of federal and state accountability, district and school leaders have had very little choice than to place a tremendous emphasis on improving student achievement through success on test scores. Through the dedicated work of leaders and teachers, many schools experienced significant improvements in test scores, hailing instant success. However, as new performance standards emerged along with new metrics for measuring school performance, many schools hit plateaus in test score results. The result has been a decline in their school ratings that often labeled them as "failing schools."

This new label has created tensions for superintendents between the relationship of schools to their communities and the need for all students to be successful. The testing metrics used in assessing the success of schools has created school environments that are disingenuous to learning. This is not an indictment on using curricular standards in a system of accountability. However, accountability systems predicated on single measures often result in district and school leaders driving initiatives that simply have not improved test scores.

Superintendents who experience the most success focus on the culture of schools with an understanding that the most gains come from the system's ability to understand the individual needs of students. Doyle (2016) asserts, "Instead of control, competition, stress, standardized testing, screen-based schools and loosened teacher qualifications, try warmth, collaboration, and highly professionalized, teacher-led encouragement and assessment" (para. 2).

BELIEFS TO PRACTICE

The major challenge superintendents' face is changing the adult beliefs about the potential of all students. Meeting this challenge underscores the realization that all students learn differently and there is a need to create varied learning opportunities for success. For all students to be successful, taking risks into the unknown is not an option. Couros (2015) is resolute, "If we are really wanting to serve our students and help them to develop to become the leaders and learners of today and the future, taking risks in our practice is not only encouraged, but necessary" (para. 5).

Superintendents must understand why students learn differently today and that their primary role as the district leader is to ensure that new instructional designs engage all students. Creating clarity and alignment of programs requires simplicity in directions, transparency in actions, and monitoring systems that enable the district to make midcourse adjustments. Effectiveness is realized when the system is clear on what they want for their students.

SHIFTING COMMUNITIES

Superintendents have a tedious and delicate path to navigate the educational terrain, given the changing demographics of communities and transient student and teacher populations. Getting school and community members to understand the changes in populations is not easy and often lags well behind the immediate challenges district leaders face. The traditional approach to these kinds of changes has been to discuss how to deal with community issues.

In the new day, superintendents need to move away from dealing with the issue of changing student populations and move toward understanding the dynamics of shifting and evolving communities. When leaders understand the problems, then the solutions have the potential for positive long-term results. Eng (2013) suggests that "The current school reform model, based on equality, is well intentioned and politically correct, but an antiquated solution for unleashing innovation since it ignores inherent demographic differences" (p. 280).

School and community leaders are best positioned to support children by understanding their community's assets. Schools cannot do it alone, but communities that have an interest in all students achieving can. In this day of often limited or competing resources, superintendents need to seek and design partnerships with organizations that can jointly engage in the work needed to support children. The work can no longer be about what organization is in control but rather creating a "shared space" where each organization can work freely and collaboratively within their organizational frameworks. When organizations work in isolation, the problems remain unresolved and students continue to be at a disadvantage.

DEVELOPING LEADERS

The role of superintendents in developing district and school leaders varies dramatically across districts. Regardless of the circumstances, superintendents have a primary responsibility for developing leaders within the system and in their communities. In the midst of all they are required to do, superintendents have a responsibility to develop building leaders who are ready to transform and sustain changes that improves student achievement. According to Hallinger (2011), principals matter second only to teachers in promoting gains in student achievement.

Leading school leaders requires the superintendent to be the lead learner in the system. This does not mean the superintendent is the ultimate expert; rather, it means the superintendent continually has an instructional focus. This focus includes having conversations and knowing the right questions to ask when meeting with principals, individually or in small or large settings. Superintendents are the instructional face of the district, and they must have the ability to activate conversations about instructional practice (Zepeda & Lanoue, 2017). If superintendents believe that instruction is central to the success of all students, then they must lead it. The development of principals and the instructional program cannot not be delegated.

Supporting and developing leaders does not stop at the schoolhouse door because "The role of the superintendent as a community leader looks far different than the role of the superintendent as the district leader" (Lanoue, 2017, para. 11). When district and school leaders enact their roles in ways to influence the leadership in their communities, then the focus moves to the needs of children both inside and outside of school. The reality is that collaboration maximizes everyone's efforts to support children.

DIGITAL LANDSCAPE

The fast evolution of the digital landscape has created a new set of opportunities for superintendents to transform schools differently to make the shift into a digital landscape. However, everyone will not readily embrace making this shift to technology. In the technology space, two opposite views exist:

1. Those who think schools have worked well by using traditional systems with minimal use of technology.
2. Those who see the digital space as an opportunity to create new systems through digital access to close the achievement gap.

If district and school leaders view the technology landscape as "doing more of the same" with new technology tools, then achievement gains will likely be less than minimal, and the impact of technology on achievement will remain modest. Darling-Hammond, Zielezinski, and Goldman's (2014) research is worth noting, "students learn more when they use technology to create new content themselves, rather than just being the recipients of content designed by others" (p. 9).

Decisions about entering the digital space will need to reflect personalization on how each student learns and acquires new skills. Traditional knowledge-driven lesson designs do little to personalize learning for students. Superintendents need to step beyond the present and the past and look more into the unknown. The digital space will provide students with access to information in ways that are very different, and this access will likely be one of the key drivers in closing the achievement gaps that exist in schools across this country.

It is important for superintendents to reflect on how access in the digital landscape can change outcomes for children. Leading in the digital space will likely be a defining moment for superintendents as educational cultures are transformed to meet the needs of students. Polyak and Lubelfeld (2016) point to the urgency of superintendents leading when they advocate that "putting student voices at the center of everything we do will help us design the future with them and for them" (para. 3).

YOUR VOICE

Superintendents are reminded daily that education in our country is entangled in control, ownership, and politics. While the federal role in education oscillates between too little or too much, its impact on school districts at the state and local levels is crippling the ability for superintendents to lead schools and their districts. Legislators at the state and federal levels that are often influenced by special interest groups have shaped educational policy and currently have the most significant impact on the future of education.

Superintendents need to assert a strong voice to influence and to take the lead in educational policy at every level. This will require courage and strong·convictions about the success and needs of all children, school transformation, and the role of communities. This role requires superintendents to understand that their sphere of influence must extend well beyond their communities. The voices of superintendents and school leaders must be personal, professional, transformative, convincing, and impactful.

DECISIONS

School districts that keep the old belief, where the center of the system consists of the school board and superintendent, will likely continue to create negative tensions in decision-making. In addition, superintendents and school boards who hold on to this level of control will likely see a significantly negative impact on school cultures, faculty and staff, and new learning initiatives. The new belief on the role of the superintendent and school board as the decision makers must shift from a focus on the school board and superintendent to a focus on meeting the expectations defined in the school district vision, mission, and beliefs that are the center of the system.

Having the vision, mission, and beliefs central to the work of the district enables the superintendent to *activate thinking rather than approve thinking*. If schools and districts are to emerge in educating students for tomorrow, it is unlikely that this will be accomplished through the individual knowledge of decision-makers alone; this will create schools for yesterday. School districts must create shared beliefs, establish committed interests, and align actions. If not, the tensions will revolve around areas explored through these questions:

1. Do the vision, mission, and beliefs create tomorrow's education or yesterday's?
2. Have we clearly defined the role of decision-makers?
3. Do decisions and actions support the district's mission and vision and beliefs or values?

Superintendents need to ask these questions to frame purpose and action around decision-making processes. Creating and sustaining positive relationships to make effective decisions requires constant attention to understanding the system's direction as well as each member's roles and responsibilities.

SOCIAL MEDIA

The influence of social media in our society can bring about either fear or opportunity. Superintendents are in a new position to rethink their communication plans and how social media can help shape the work of their districts. While traditional communication plans of the past have helped districts disseminate information on the workings of their systems, superintendents must be aware that social media now allows systems to go far beyond one-way information systems.

Superintendents must see social media as an opportunity by understanding its importance and its pitfalls because "Social networks are one of the fastest growing industries in the world" (Social Media, 2017, para. 5). Most school districts initially viewed social media as a vehicle for transparency in information flow and to reach a larger audience for messaging and branding the system. Now, social media tools go deeper in influencing school decisions at every level.

Social media is a critical element for superintendents to engage their own systems as well as to engage outside stakeholders in the efforts to transform district systems. Social media outlets can help superintendents with developing and adopting innovations, creating two-way conversations that provide immediate feedback, and generating greater ownership by all stakeholders (Telio, 2016). Whether school leaders are social media users or not, they must develop a plan that embraces its importance and value in shaping the future of education.

BALANCE

Leadership in and of itself is extremely challenging and taxing. However, the job of school superintendents today has expanded in scope and complexity. According to Chingos, Whitehurst, and Lindquist (2014), the "school district superintendent is largely a short-term job. The typical superintendent has been in the job for three to four years" (p. 1). Following the trail of attrition, Becca Bracy Knight, executive director for the Broad Center for the Management of School Systems, when interviewed by Freedberg and Collier (2016), stated:

> I don't think nearly enough superintendents have the time to make both dramatic and lasting improvements in their districts. We have to ask ourselves what is keeping people from staying in their jobs longer. If you want big change, and big improvements for your students, and you want it to be sustainable, that simply takes time. (para. 6)

For superintendents, the bottom line is they must be balanced in their personal and professional lives if they want to stay healthy and engaged to do the work required over time.

Developing the skills that superintendents need in balancing their lives will not get easier as the work load increases and the demands of accountability continue to change and weigh on systems. However, superintendents must be able to reflect on their work and have the support required to reconcile the many philosophical underpinnings of the decisions they make for the system and their communities. Healthy and balanced superintendents lead healthy and balanced systems for the long-term.

SUMMARY

The responsibilities given to superintendents continue to increase and expand well beyond the day-to-day decisions in "running" a school district. Superintendents now assume leadership roles that affect both students and adults in their schools and in their communities. Shaping school and community cultures so all students are successful requires superintendents to put in place new systems that are developed with a clear direction founded on its beliefs, and monitored at every level—all with a relentless focus on improving the learning experiences for all students to be successful in *their* ever changing world.

However, with all the decisions required in creating new systems and processes, superintendents need to ensure that the system has coherence. Coherence is the alignment of system actions, its direction established by its vision, mission, and beliefs, and the impact on every student. Chapter 2 examines how districts can approach coherence through monitoring processes and feedback systems designed to ensure the district is moving in the intended direction to get the desired results.

SUGGESTED READINGS

Chaudry, A., Morrissey, T., Weiland, C., & Yoshikawa, H. (2017). *Cradle to kindergarten: A new plan to combat inequality*. New York, NY: Russell Sage Foundation.

Koretz, D. (2017). *The testing charade: Pretending to make schools better*. Chicago, IL: University of Chicago Press.

Lubelfeld, M., & Polyak, N. (2017). *The unlearning leader: Leading for tomorrow's schools today*. Lanham, MD: Rowman & Littlefield.

Merrow, J. (2017). *Addicted to reform: A 12-Step program to rescue public education*. New York, NY: The New Press.

REFERENCES

Chingos, M. M., Whitehurst, G. J., & Lindquist, K. M. (2014). *School superintendents: Vital or irrelevant?* Washington, DC: Brown Center of Education Policy at Brookings. Retrieved from https://www.brookings.edu/wp-content/uploads/2016/06/SuperintendentsBrown-Center9314.pdf

Couros, G. (2014, November 16). Educational leadership philosophy. [Blog]. *The Principal of Change.* Retrieved from https://georgecouros.ca/blog/about-me/educational-leadership-philosophy

Couros, G. (2015, July 11). The importance of taking risks. [Blog]. *The Principal of Change: Stories of Learning and Leading.* Retrieved from https://georgecouros.ca/blog/archives/5402

Darling-Hammond, L., Zielezinski, M. B., & Goldman, S. (2014). *Using technology to support at-risk students' learning.* Stanford, CA: Stanford Center for Opportunity Policy in Education and Washington, DC: Alliance for Excellent Education. Retrieved from https://edpolicy.stanford.edu/sites/default/files/scope-pub-using-technology-report.pdf

Doyle, W. (2016). How Finland broke every rule—and created a top school system. [Blog]. *The Hechinger Report.* Retrieved from http://hechingerreport.org/how-finland-broke-every-rule-and-created-a-top-school-system/

Eng, N. (2013). The impact of demographics on 21st century education. *Society, 50*(3), 272–282. doi: 10.1007/s12115-013-9655-z

Freedberg, L., & Collier, M. (2016, November 6). Districts grapple with superintendent turnover with new reforms. *EdSource.* Retrieved from https://edsource.org/2016/districts-grapple-with-superintendent-turnover-along-with-new-reforms/571804

Hallinger, P. (2011). Leadership for learning: Lessons from 40 years of empirical research. *Journal of Educational Administration, 49*(2), 125–142. doi:10.1108/09578231111116699

Hirsh, S., Psencik, K., & Brown, F. (2014). *Becoming a learning system.* Oxford, OH: Learning Forward.

Lanoue, P. D. (2017, October 6). Leading beyond the boundaries of schools. [Blog]. Course Correction. TrustED. Retrieved from http://trustedk12.com/leading-beyond-the-boundaries-of-school/

Polyak, N., & Lubelfeld, M. (2016, December 15). How school superintendents explored the future of learning together. [Blog]. Chicago, IL: The School Superintendents Association Digital Consortium. Retrieved from https://www.blog.google/topics/education/how-school-superintendents-explored-future-learning-together/

Social Media. (2017). Why you need to understand the importance of social media. [Blog]. Growth Gurus. Retrieved from https://www.growthgurus.com/blog/business-brand-need-understand-importance-social-media/

Telio, S. (2016, January 19). *How to collect customer feedback using social media.* [Blog]. Build on Purpose. Retrieved from https://community.uservoice.com/blog/customer-feedback-social-media/

Zepeda, S. J., & Lanoue, P. D. (2017). Conversation walks: Improving instructional leadership. *Educational Leadership*, *74*(8), 58–61. Retrieved from http://www.ascd.org/publications/educational-leadership/may17/vol74/num08/Conversation-Walks@-Improving-Instructional-Leadership.aspx

Chapter 2

Coherence in a System of Change

IN THIS CHAPTER . . .

- Vision, Mission, and Beliefs Guide Strategic Planning and Practices
- Aligning the Strategic Plan to the Work
- Developing a Common Instructional Language
- Performance Plans for District Divisions
- Improvement Planning for Schools
- Creating Effective Models for Monitoring

LETTER FROM THE SUPERINTENDENT

Dear System Principals:

I am developing the calendar for this year's performance checks that will begin in January. Like the past year, each performance check should be designed for one hour and fifteen minutes. I expect that your school improvement team and all active participants will be present for this review process.

Please remember that I am looking at both the processes in place by the school improvement teams to monitor the initiatives at the schools as well as a midterm summary of key successes and areas that need greater focus. While I expect to have structure to give time for adequate discussion, I also anticipate that the informality in drilling down and fleshing out vital details will also add to our conversation.

I look forward to our meeting to discuss your initiatives in support of the district's strategic plan and your progress to improve the performance of our

students. Thank you for what you do every day for our students and for your
relentless efforts to influence the lives of our students.
Sincerely,
Superintendent

From a systems view, creating coherence between the school district's direction, as defined through its vision, mission, and beliefs, and the direct and indirect actions that affect students rests squarely on the shoulders of the superintendent. Most districts experience intense tensions when there is misalignment between the systems or when districts do not have a clear direction. Often these tensions emerge quickly when a strategic plan finds the evaluation of existing programs or the creation of new ones that are unknown or unfamiliar to the system. If systems want to transform to meet the varying needs of students for tomorrow's world, healthy tensions will be created (Zepeda, Lanoue, Price, & Jimenez, 2014).

Coherence in the system begins with the vision, mission, beliefs, and strategic plan that serve as a blueprint for all the work in the system, especially change. When there is coherence, a more robust strategic plan can support changes. No longer can we fall back to the old focus where the school board and superintendent are at the center of the system. The new focus is where the vision, mission, beliefs, and strategic plan center the work of the system (Zepeda, Lanoue, Creel, & Price, 2016).

Coherence requires a working understanding of all elements of the system from the board level to the impact on every student in the system. According to Githens (2013), effective strategic plans make sense; however, ineffective ones reflect a compilation of unconnected actions and activities from multiple divisions, and the efforts to meet goals often polarize personnel across divisions.

The primacy of the work of the superintendent rests on ensuring clarity and transparency, and this responsibility cannot be delegated. Superintendents must ensure that there is coherence and monitoring strategies to support the alignment of district processes. Nagy and Fawcett (n.d.) share that "developing effective vision and mission statements are two of the most important tasks your organization will ever do, because almost everything else you do will be affected by these statements" (n.p.).

VISION, MISSION, AND BELIEFS GUIDE
STRATEGIC PLANNING AND PRACTICES

District vision, mission, and beliefs not only need to be visible and readily accessible, but they must also drive the aspirations, purposes, and existence of your district. The vision and mission create a picture in concise statements about the organization's aspirations and its actions. However, these statements and corresponding processes in developing them cannot be relegated to posters on the wall and the bylines on the system's web pages. Districts experience great disconnects and stunted growth when their vision, mission, and beliefs do not drive strategic planning, program decisions, and processes.

The vision provides a framework to answer questions on "why" the district makes certain decisions in their planning. The mission answers the question of "what" the district will do. Without defining the aspirations and actions of the district about its children, districts will not successfully engage in the transformations and innovations through their strategic planning that are needed to affect every student in the district. Miller (2014) illustrates the connection, "what is the strategy trying to achieve if not the company mission? And what is the mission if not an embodiment of the vision?" (n.p.)

School boards that develop vision, mission, and beliefs for the system are the best positioned to make the most effective decisions in all aspects of the district to develop schools for tomorrow and not for today. Districts will need to engage in a process where the needs, values, and actions that support the uniqueness of the community are discussed and understood.

A comprehensive process of developing the vision and mission is vital if the district has the desire to be innovative in the redesign of curriculum, implementation and refinement of programs, and infusion of new and emerging technologies.

While beliefs are often incorporated as part of the vision, beliefs can stand alone and form the fundamental values for the work of the district. Beliefs are the connectors that join the "heart" of the school community with the "heart" of the community at large to create one strong voice for all children to be successful. Core beliefs "define and create culture and act as touchstones to guide behavior" (Brady, n.d., para. 17). To create schools for all children, the beliefs must support changes that explore new ways of engaging them by moving away from traditional practices. Beliefs allow the system and community to take risks with children that can take them to places they never thought they could be.

Reflecting on the Work

With your vision, mission, and beliefs . . .

1. Identify the processes in place to ensure practice aligns with your district's beliefs. If there are practices that do not align, what types of efforts are needed to get them to align?
2. What evidence do you have that your vision, mission, and beliefs are understood and drive the system?

ALIGNING THE STRATEGIC PLAN TO THE WORK

Once the district has an agreed-on vision, mission, and beliefs, the superintendent now takes the lead role in developing the district strategic plan for approval by the school board. Effective strategic planning accomplishes three primary objectives (Lannon, 2015):

- Ensure strong connection among the organization's mission and its operational resources.
- Fine tune departmental goals and objectives and discover implementation gaps.
- Address issues that may exist around internal efficiencies and effectiveness. (n.p.)

Developing the strategic plan is not just setting performance targets with broadly stated goals. While strategic plans across systems may look different, they all typically include the district's vision, mission and beliefs, long- and/or short-term goals, objectives, initiatives that drive action plans, and metrics to measure the work.

System goals do not need to be a cast of one hundred, but rather several who drive the system in the direction that has been defined and predicated on where it wants to go and how it wants to make the journey. In addition, strategic plans should include performance objectives as well as initiatives or actions that narrows the focus of the work and establishes greater definitions allowing the organization to design its work at all levels. Sage (n.d.) suggests key attributes for effective strategic plans:

- Purpose-driven: A plan based on a mission and a real, true competitive advantage is key. Without it, what's the point of the plan or the organization?
- Integrated: Each element supports the next. No objectives are disconnected from goals, and no strategies sit all alone.
- Systemic: Don't think of the plan as one big document. Instead, give it life by breaking it into executable parts.
- Dynamic: The plan is not a static document but a living one.
- Holistic: All areas of the organization are included. Don't plan based on departments first because you risk limiting your thinking. Plan by thinking about the organization as a whole entity and then implement on a department-by-department basis.
- Understandable: Everyone gets it. If anyone, from the top of the organization to the bottom, doesn't understand the plan or how he or she fits in, it won't work.

- Realistic: You can implement the plan. Don't over plan. Make sure you have the resources to support the goals you decide to focus on. (para. 4)

The objectives of the strategic plan may define either processes or specific outcomes. Developing clear and measurable objectives is vital to the strategic planning process and may be assessed either quantitatively or qualitatively.

Typically, system divisions (Instruction, Human Resources, District Services, etc.) are intensely involved in developing performance objectives that they believe support the system's direction from the work in their respective areas. Superintendents need to go one step further and engage in processes to ensure that each division's goals collectively support the work needed, as defined by its vision and mission.

Operationalizing the collective work of divisions occurs by developing district initiatives that support performance objectives as well as the actions of each division. It is here that systems can effectively overlap efforts and resources within the district and community. While writing initiatives, keep in mind that:

- Multiple initiatives should be developed to support a performance objective.
- Multiple divisions may develop initiatives for one performance objective.
- Initiatives are to be developed to change the culture of the system and are not already part of the existing culture.
- Completion of initiatives may take several years.
- Initiatives are written to ensure results—the impact on student performance.
- Initiatives are not part of the division's required responsibilities.
- Initiatives use specific language that is understood and not defined using acronyms.

Textbox 2.2 is an example of the alignment of initiatives or actions to a performance objective related to developing trauma-informed practices (see chapter 3 for trauma informed practices).

Textbox 2.2. Illustrative Divisional Initiative Aligned to Performance Objectives

Performance Objective: Develop trauma-informed practices in collaboration with community agencies to support the health children require for them to be academically and socially successful.
Initiative: Identify physical health—and mental health—related barriers to learning, and partner with community agencies to provide wraparound support services.
Initiative: Prepare students and school personnel to recognize, understand and manage personal, school-wide, and/or community crises through education, interventions, and standard crisis response protocols for individuals and groups.

Initiatives may first be developed from individual divisions, but there must be a next step where multiple divisions come together and collectively review initiatives to determine effectiveness as a whole and to align divisional actions as illustrated in textbox 2.3.

Textbox 2.3. Illustrative Divisional Actions Aligned to Initiatives

Initiative: Create opportunities for classified and certified employees to earn certifications, endorsements, and education degrees through partnerships with colleges and universities that have accredited education programs.
Human Resources: Establish collaborations with universities and technical colleges to offer full access to postsecondary programs for certification and endorsements.
Instructional Services: Create opportunity for current teachers to earn endorsements in other areas (i.e., Reading, Gifted, ESOL, math, and science).

If what the district says it will do does not affect students in every seat and in every classroom, then the problem lies with the adults in the system, with the ultimate responsibility resting with the superintendent. Throughout every aspect of the strategic planning process, the superintendent needs to inspire leaders and hold themselves and teams accountable rather than inform leaders and hold them accountable (Zepeda et al., 2016).

Reflecting on the Work

How does your strategic plan . . .

1. Support and guide the work of district divisions and school improvement teams?
2. Include processes for monitoring, evaluating, and modifying the strategic plan?

DEVELOPING A COMMON INSTRUCTIONAL LANGUAGE

Every school district plan must support the effectiveness of its instructional program. One of the major pitfalls for superintendents in aligning this work lies in not creating an agreed-upon and defined set of instructional practices that are the core of district programs. Schooling, Toth, and Marzano (2013) recommend that districts create a common instructional design to "provide a framework for a way to talk about instruction that is shared by everyone" (p. 1). Moreover,

> Principals and teachers [must] use a common language of instruction to converse about effective teaching, give and receive feedback, collect and act upon data to monitor growth regarding the reasoned use of the strategies

identified in the framework, and align professional development needs against the framework. (p. 1)

Schools can become divided and inconsistent when core instructional practices are not clearly understood. Core instructional practices should be developed using a common nomenclature with clarity in its design and implementation. Agreement and understanding of instructional practice changes the focus of the superintendent from one where all students *can* learn to one where all students *must* learn (Zepeda & Lanoue, 2017).

One of the most challenging expressions used by a superintendent is that it is "not negotiable." However, if schools are going to align their system to core beliefs, aspects of the organization cannot be negotiated or mitigated. In addition, superintendents and leaders cannot commit to the use of effective practices when there is little understanding about what these practices would look like in their system.

Districts and schools can create coherence in their programs and become more effective when there are commitments to instructional practices that are held by all without exception. These practices or commitments must be agreed upon, clearly understood, and pervasively used across the system. Textbox 2.5 provides one example of a commitment to system-wide practices and examples of what they might look like when observed.

Textbox 2.5. Sample Commitment with Related Observable Practices

Commitment: Personalizing learning for every student by identifying individual learning needs using multiple data sources.
Observable Practices:

- Teacher teams develop lesson plans that reflect individual learning needs using data on performance and student learning attributes.
- Performance data are used to adapt a lesson or strategy if instruction is not working for a student, or to offer new challenges for students who have mastered the learning objectives.
- Teachers disaggregate performance data using learning technologies to understand students' learning needs.
- Student work is collected, analyzed, shared, and archived.

Adapted from Zepeda (2017)

Creating the highest level of agreement about instructional practice is paramount to aligning the system. This process can take on many forms with varying products, but in the end, students, teachers, and leaders must be able to describe in-depth their practice and the commonalities across the district. Alignment of the system is realized when all members of the organization understand the expectations that are steadfast and not negotiable, especially regarding instructional and school-level practices.

Reflecting on the Work
In understanding a common instructional language . . . 1. What instructional expectations in your system are not negotiable? 2. Would students transferring within the system have similar classroom experiences across schools?

PERFORMANCE PLANS FOR DISTRICT DIVISIONS

The district office is not an entity that is "in and of itself" but rather one that must be organized to support the work of schools—its leaders, teachers, parents, and community. The functions of district office divisions change, and these functions become clearer when their work is aligned to the goals, performance objectives, and initiatives defined by the strategic plan. The transformation of district offices recommended by Honig (2013) requires a substantive shift in the focus and alignment of the work from strategic planning to what is required for principals to improve performance in their buildings. Moreover, district office and school-based leaders must work collaboratively as described by Honig (2013), to include:

- Intensive partnerships between executive-level central office staff and school principals that aim to help principals grow as instructional leaders. These partnerships elevate responsibility for supporting principal growth to a position in one or two levels beyond the superintendent's office.
- Completely redesigning each central office function for performance. Such redesign involves each unit working with various data to identify a defined set of high-quality, relevant services for schools—those likely to help schools build their capacity for excellent teaching and learning.
- Performance-oriented leadership on the part of the superintendent and others throughout the central office. (p. 4)

Superintendents cannot expect existing programs to grow and develop as well as initiate new ones without the strong leadership and collective planning of all divisions working in tandem with site-level leaders.

Ensuring that division performance plans align to the defined work of the district, which in turn supports the work of schools, should be primary to the leadership responsibilities of the superintendent and divisional leaders of the district. However, simply directing divisions to have a plan falls short of the mark. Superintendents and leaders need to create processes where divisional plans that include all departments support the strategic plan and aligned themselves to the district's direction.

Every division should engage in a process to develop performance plans that define the actions for district initiatives or actions that can be influenced by their work responsibilities. Districts can use common performance planning templates to better align the work, to provide a common framework that supports effective monitoring, and to frame critical conversations. Planning templates should be explicit on performance objectives, performance targets, initiatives, actions, resources, artifacts, and metrics for monitoring and evaluating.

Through these processes, superintendents can take advantage of the information and create opportunities to explore new ways to develop policies and programs that support the work of divisions. Existing systems emerge with greater clarity and new innovative systems are created when district level divisions think differently about their work, as it is aligned to well-developed district goals and accompanying initiatives.

Superintendents need to understand how the actions of every district division and related departments support schools through their actions that align to the strategic plan. Well-designed and well-written divisional improvement plans align to the district's focus about what is important, provide direction in the allocation of resources, and assist in developing critical monitoring processes. When district office divisional plans are aligned to the goals and objectives of the strategic plan, then schools are able to create local improvement plans that are supported in ways very different than the traditional hands-off district office.

Reflecting on the Work
In providing direction for divisional work . . . 1. How do divisions determine their yearly goals and work schedule? 2. What indicators do you use to ensure the work of a district office is connected to the improvement work at the school level?

IMPROVEMENT PLANNING FOR SCHOOLS

Principals must be the lead reformer and transformer in their schools, therefore assuming full responsibility for directing all school improvement initiatives. Louis, Leithwood, Wahlstrom, and Anderson (2010) underscore that effective principals work with teachers by actively engaging in:

- Focusing the school on goals and expectations for student achievement.
- Attending to teachers' professional development needs.
- Creating structures and opportunities for teacher collaboration. (p. 2)

Rigorous school improvement efforts require principals to have a skill set to understand the dynamics of school improvement.

Giving the needed support and professional development for school leaders is the primary responsibility of the superintendent and district leaders. When superintendents become the lead learner, they can model the expected leader skills and more importantly, the dispositions needed to lead learning. The superintendent and district-level leaders must work purposefully to know and understand the culture and performance of schools and then be able to support principals in their growth in leading school improvement.

Principals' improvement efforts begin by creating School Improvement Leadership Teams (SILT) that develop and monitor the school improvement efforts. SILT teams typically include teachers, leaders, and support personnel. However, principals may decide that other members of the school community are important in the improvement process and become part of the team. SILT teams should include a broad representation of the school community whose members are ready and willing to assume leadership roles.

SILT teams are trained annually in analyzing data, identifying effective school-focused strategies, and using monitoring processes. School-based leadership teams meet throughout the year to establish school improvement initiatives, monitor school progress, modify initiatives, and ensure school-based practices result in meeting their targeted outcomes.

The district may select common focus areas to address a system-wide deficiency. As an example, the district may have a focus on mathematics; therefore, all schools would have an initiative on how to improve student achievement in mathematics. The School Improvement Plan (SIP) would have detail on how each initiative affects mathematics achievement and its implementation. When using a district-wide focus, a common metric for evaluation would be established for monitoring and evaluation.

The SIP is part of a comprehensive cycle that requires involvement at every level in the district. To monitor continuity across all schools, districts should consider developing specific tools and processes to provide continuous feedback on individual SIPs and to monitor their progress in meeting goals. In addition, similar to central office divisions, formal and informal monitoring processes should be established including performance checks scheduled during the year with every school improvement team to determine progress, areas of strength, and areas for growth.

The most important factor to ensure coherence of the SIP is establishing conversations that are pervasive at every level and where monitoring processes become as important as the outcomes. School improvement plans drive the work of individual schools; however, the plans are tightly aligned to the district direction with clarity in each action step. All school improvement plans detail how school and/or system personnel will monitor and report results.

Because principals hold the primary responsibility for school improvement, much of their work is evaluated by their success in developing, implementing, and monitoring the school improvement of their schools. Alignment of the job expectations for principals is inextricably connected to the work of school improvement teams.

Reflecting on the Work
In planning for school improvement . . .   1. Do schools annually develop school performance or improvement plans?   2. How are leaders supported during this process?

CREATING EFFECTIVE MODELS FOR MONITORING

Superintendents have the responsibility to know that "what they say is occurring is actually occurring" and this analysis is not a simple or random process. We know that monitoring what you expect is a critical element of effective strategic planning. However, monitoring processes are more than a formal report or simply an event. Effective monitoring requires both formal and informal processes. Superintendents need to be very deliberate in how information is gathered and reported across the district. Every conversation, whether at a formal administrative meeting or in more informal settings, provides invaluable information for assessing the coherence of the system as well as identifying areas where adjustments need to be made quickly.

District Monitoring

At the district level, aligning the work of divisions to the strategic plan not only affects the effectiveness of the central office but also models the expected behaviors and establishes the groundwork for the success of school leaders. Regardless of the size of organizations, processes for monitoring need to be in place to align the work with expected outcomes. Process monitoring should include steps for feedback on division plans, as they are developed, regular internal divisional reviews and summative reviews that may include members from outside of the division.

For formal divisional reviews, inclusion of principals or other members of a district's team can play an important role not only in providing feedback, but also in closing the gap between the perceived role of the central office and actual practice. Typically, when principals are included in this process, the role of the central office is viewed as supportive and responsive to school needs rather than simply a monitoring strategy.

Informal divisional reviews should occur regularly across the system. These can be done through teacher, principal, and district-level conversations, classroom visits, professional learning, and by attending planning meetings with various groups. As an example, if instructional services have a performance goal to improve instructional practices and provide an aligned and challenging curriculum, then district leaders can gain great insight through these types of conversations in schools. Information from informal processes "fill the gaps" often not found in formal types of reviews.

Formal reviews provide key benchmarks for leaders and their departments on progress, mainly because these types of reviews are evidence-driven and directly connected to initiatives and performance goals. At least once a year, often at the midterm, each division should have a comprehensive review with the superintendent and/or key division leaders. Though formal in its design, this review does not need to have a script by the presenters. It can be more like a focused conversation (with all key members of the divisions) about the rationale for each initiative, the processes used by each division to monitor implementation, and the results to determine effectiveness.

School Level Monitoring

At the school level, principals play the "critical" role in leading and monitoring their school improvement initiatives. They must be instructional leaders by creating conversations that occur across the school to forward improvement processes. Establishing well-developed improvement plans with understood actions and clear metrics for assessment that are aligned to district goals is paramount in getting the wanted results. This does not mean that initiatives may not differ across schools; however, the result (what do you want to accomplish?) for all students in the district does not change.

Not every principal enters the job with all the skills to lead school improvement; however, with support and unified understanding of school improvement, along with leadership across the district, and with district support, principals gain the skills and confidence to succeed in this role. Establishing improvement summits where leaders from across the district come together to analyze achievement data and engage in conversations about initiatives that can address areas of concern are extremely beneficial and provide professional learning in the field. School leaders collaborating on performance establish a culture that we are all in this together.

Like district divisions, school improvement plans and local initiatives need review and feedback in their development to improve alignment and to monitor. Critical in this process is the review of the plan at the beginning of its development to ensure alignment to the strategic plan, clarity of the initiatives, effectiveness of implementation steps, and metrics for evaluating results. Key questions that help district teams provide feedback, so schools can further develop their improvement plans include:

- Do the performance targets align to the district performance targets and/or do they align to the focus areas (i.e., math, reading, technology use, etc.)?
- Do the performance targets identify specific subgroups?
- Are the performance targets aggressive in a way that will close achievement gaps?
- Are initiatives written as action statements?
- Can staff, parents, and community members understand the initiatives?
- Does the plan establish relevant artifacts and evidence in its monitoring?
- How does the plan outline professional learning for teachers and leaders?

Once reviewed, SILT teams are then responsible for implementing initiatives and monitoring both their implementation and performance results. SILT teams should meet twice a month at a minimum, and record the status of each initiative as well as modifications to the plan. Again, both formal and informal conversations across the school community play a critical role in the SILT's effectiveness in leading school improvement.

Maintaining a focus on the work requires a comprehensive structure with defined processes that ensures formal and informal conversations and reporting to occur at all levels of the organization. Both system and school improvement efforts become compromised when school leaders fail to understand the elements of developing improvement planning coupled with the need for focused monitoring processes. Table 2.1 provides a framework for monitoring effective SIPs.

Finally, a more formal process referred to here as "performance checks" provide an opportunity for district leaders to interact with SILT teams about the effectiveness of their school improvement plans and the processes used to monitor and modify each initiative. In this process, it is important to discuss the process of monitoring to minimize the thinking that SILT teams need to provide a "big" report. Performance checks should assess the totality of the

Table 2.1. Framework for Monitoring Effective School Improvement Processes

1	Alignment with District Strategic Plan
2	District and School Level Performance Data Reviews (Data Summits)
3	Incorporate District Focus Areas into School Plans
4	Leadership Work Sessions in Data Analysis and School Improvement Initiatives
5	Define the Work of School-Level Improvement Teams
6	School Improvement Plan Reviews and Feedback from the District Level
7	School-Level Progress Monitoring
8	Midterm (or more) Performance Checks by District Teams
9	Final Review Based on Year-End Performance
10	Repeat Cycle

work by the SILT teams, how these teams implemented new strategies, and monitored changes in the school.

Reflecting on the Work
In your district monitoring system . . .   1. As superintendent, what is your involvement in design and implementation of district- and school-level school improvement planning?   2. How confident are you in describing the school improvement practices in your district?

SUMMARY

Creating district coherence requires the adults in the system to design and implement monitoring systems around a clearly understood instructional framework using improvement plans at every level to support the district's strategic plan. System coherence is established by using data from multiple sources to determine effectiveness and to make adjustments.

Establishing coherence in the system requires complex system processes that become even more difficult as the needs of children and families change. Moving from most students being successful to all students being successful in today's world will require a greater understanding of community dynamics, with specific focus on the health, social, and emotional needs of students and their families. Chapter 3 introduces new perspectives on how schools will need to become involved in the overall health of their children and communities if they are to be responsive to every student's learning needs.

A SUPERINTENDENT'S DIVE INTO SYSTEM COHERENCE

1. Draw an imaginary line between district performance objectives and students in the district, and assess the level of alignment from the district level to the school level.
2. Create conversations with several principals and SILT members to determine their roles in school improvement planning.
3. Write a one-page letter to your community on how the strategic plan drives school improvement efforts to support the learning experience for all children.

SUGGESTED READINGS

Anderson, S., Mascall, B., Stiegelbauer, S., & Park, J. (2012). No one way: Differentiating school district leadership and support for school improvement. *Journal of Educational Change, 13*(4), 403–430. doi: 10.1007/s10833-012-9189-y

Lindahl, R. A., & Beach, R. H. (2013). The role of evaluation in the school improvement process. *Planning & Changing, 44*(1/2), 56–72. Retrieved from https://education.illinoisstate.edu/planning/

Supovitz, J. A., & Spillane, J. P. (2015). *Challenging standards: Navigating conflict and building capacity in the era of the Common Core*. Lanham, MD: Rowman & Littlefield.

REFERENCES

Brady, S. (n.d.). Vision, mission and core beliefs. *Prism Decision Systems*. Retrieved from https://www.prismdecision.com/schoolutions/vision-mission-core-beliefs/

Githens, G. (2013). Coherence: It is only a good plan (strategy) if it makes good sense. *Leading Strategic Initiatives*. Retrieved from https://leadingstrategicinitiatives.com/2013/12/31/coherence-it-is-only-a-good-plan-strategy-if-it-makes-good-sense/

Honig, M. I. (2013). *From tinkering to transformation: Strengthening school district central office performance*. American Enterprise Institute Outlook Series, 4, 1–10. Washington, DC: American Enterprise Institute for Public Policy Research.

Lannon, R. (2015). Four steps to align your organization to its strategic plan. *PM Times—Resources for project managers*. Retrieved from https://www.projecttimes.com/articles/four-steps-to-align-your-organization-to-its-strategic-plan.html

Louis, K. S., Leithwood, K., Wahlstrom, K. L., & Anderson, S. E. (2010). Learning from leadership: Investigating the links to improved student learning. *Knowledge in Brief: Findings You Can Use from New Wallace Research*, 1–4. New York, NY: Wallace Foundation. Retrieved from www.wallacefoundation.org

Miller, B. (2014). Strategy, mission, and vision: How do they all fit together? *HR Daily Advisor*. Retrieved from http://hrdailyadvisor.blr.com/2014/09/09/strategy-mission-and-vision-how-do-they-all-fit-together/

Nagy, J., & Fawcett, S. B. (n.d.). Proclaiming your dream: Developing vision and mission statements. In J. Nagy & S. B. Fawcett (Eds.), *Developing a strategic plan and organizational structure*. Chapter 8 Sections: Section 2. Retrieved from http://ctb.ku.edu/en/table-of-contents/structure/strategic-planning/vision-mission-statements/main

Sage, S. (n.d.). Key elements on how to write a strategic plan. *On Strategy*. Retrieved from https://onstrategyhq.com/resources/key-elements-on-how-to-write-a-strategic-plan/

Schooling, P., Toth, M., & Marzano, R. (2013). The critical importance of a common language of instruction. Blairsville, PA: Learning Sciences Marzano Center: Teacher and Leader Evaluation. Retrieved from https://www.learningsciences.com/wp/wp-content/uploads/2017/06/Common-Language-of-Instruction-2013.pdf

Zepeda, S. J. (2017). *Instructional supervision: Applying tools and concepts* (4th ed.). New York, NY: Routledge.

Zepeda, S. J., & Lanoue, P. D. (2017). Conversation walks: Improving instructional leadership. *Educational Leadership*, *74*(8), 58–61. Retrieved from http://www.ascd.org/publications/educational-leadership/may17/vol74/num08/Conversation-Walks@-Improving-Instructional-Leadership.aspx

Zepeda, S. J., Lanoue, P. D., Creel, W. G., & Price, N. F. (2016). Supervising and evaluating principals—The new work of superintendents and central office personnel. In J. Glanz & S. J. Zepeda (Eds.), *Supervision: New perspectives for theory and practice* (pp. 63–79). Lanham, MD: Rowman & Littlefield.

Zepeda, S. J., Lanoue, P. D., Price, N. F., & Jimenez, A. M. (2014). Principal evaluation—Linking individual and building-level progress: Making the connections and embracing the tensions. *School Leadership & Management*, *34*(4), 324–351. doi:10.1080/13632434.2014.928681

Chapter 3

Leading in Shifting Landscapes

IN THIS CHAPTER . . .

- Shifting Needs of Communities
- Shared Space and Collaborating Beyond the System
- Risks If Systems Remain Static

LETTER FROM THE SUPERINTENDENT

Dear President of the Chamber of Commerce:

First and foremost, thank you and the Chamber for your continued support and engagement in educating our children and young adults. I believe our conversation last week about the partnership with the Chamber Board was both informative and insightful. It was evident from our meeting that both of our organizations viewed this initiative as one that would benefit not only our youth in the community but also our businesses as well.

To recap our conversation, we want to create a new model that involves multiple businesses and manufacturers in our city. We are very interested in developing a unique collaboration between our school district and businesses with a focus on youth development, youth education, and career goal attainment.

The program would be tailored to meet the individual needs of young adults through varied work experiences that enable them to have educational and work choices upon graduation from high school. Through our partnership, all areas of the business and manufacturing communities can support our youth development—which is a primary focus of county agencies, including

the Mayor's Youth Development Task Force, Area Chamber of Commerce,
faith-based organizations, and local businesses.
   I look forward to the reflections by the Chamber as we co-construct a
model that will serve our students and community well.
Sincerely,
Superintendent

   The history of public education in our country has left a trail of reforms
and transformations with the most recent being the No Child Left Behind
Act of 2001, reauthorized by the Every Student Succeeds Act of 2015. While
critics, including many superintendents across the country, often cringe
when speaking of accountability linked to high-stakes testing, one point of
agreement is the focus on every individual student. While these reforms are
not perfect in their design, they have brought a needed urgency to understand
subgroup performance that has led to new opportunities for many students
who were often marginalized.
   The success of schools will be shaped by their understanding of shifting
populations, changes in workforce needs, injection of fast changing technologies, and unprecedented shifts in the racial and ethnic compositions of
our students and the communities that we serve. Superintendents will need to
assume an elevated role in leading their districts in forming new relationships
that help guide and support the needs of students. Colleges and universities, government agencies, and business, manufacturing, and nonprofit
organizations will be essential partners in creating "shared space" with a laser
focus on developing youth.
   Community partnerships in this shared space need the collective focus to
be on the youth of the community, supported through the missions of their
organizations. Districts can no longer be autonomous in their approach to
educating all students and must rely on the assets of their communities.
Collaborative partnerships extending outside of the walls of schools requires
superintendents to move from maintaining and leading current systems to
creating and leading new systems.

SHIFTING NEEDS OF COMMUNITIES

Realizing the composition of the communities served by their schools
will bring additional requirements for understanding to the work of
superintendents. The racial and ethnic shifts can no longer be ignored or
acknowledged without change in school focus, programming, and practices
to support children. In addition, schools are experiencing shifts in the
backgrounds of students with high rates of poverty and social trauma. These

shifts require schools to change to meet the needs of children, rather than children changing to meet the needs of the school.

With the focus on improving public education, the conversations about the needs and changes occurring in families and community remains almost absent. While superintendents should never—and this means never—excuse the reason for poor performance on outside factors, they must understand the changing dynamics of their communities. Without this understanding, leading schools will be compromised to the detriment of success for *all* students in their districts, in their communities, and into life as they complete their education.

The commitment all school districts should make is that when kids walk through the school doors, we will "get it right!" When students struggle in their own lives, the learning experiences created in every classroom can be shattered in seconds when teachers, school leaders, and district leaders do not get it right. For this reason, aligning systems beliefs with actions becomes critical.

Districts improve the performance and lives of children when they create policies, develop procedures, and hire and develop adults to understand the total needs of children. Superintendents champion addressing the needs of students by knocking down barriers that stand in the way of their physical, emotional, and academic success. We must understand how their community, social, and family environments impact success. Pressing issues are universal across urban, rural, and suburban systems.

Homelessness

Homelessness is an epidemic problem and schools must be able to muster resources and personnel to support children. The statistics report that over 3.5 million people experience homelessness each year, and approximately 35 percent of the homeless population are families with children, which is the fastest growing segment of the homeless population (National Center for Homeless Education, 2015).

There are many examples of family and community factors that impact children, but less obvious to the public is student homelessness. To underscore the need for schools to recognize, support, and reach out to homeless students, the data are sobering:

> More than 1 million public school students in the United States have no room to call their own, no desk to do their homework, no bed to rely on at night. State data collection, required by federal law and aggregated by the National Center for Homeless Education, shows the number of homeless students has doubled in the past decade, to 1.3 million in 2013–2014. (Kamenetz, 2016, para. 3)

First, leaders need to understand the definition of homelessness and that being homeless is much broader than the typical imagery the media portrays, where families are living out of a car or on the streets. As reported in a 2016 U.S. Department of Education publication, *Supporting the Success of Homeless Children and Youths*, the federal McKinney-Vento Homeless Assistance Act (2010), defines homelessness as a person "who lack[s] a fixed, regular and adequate nighttime residence," (p. 2) including children who find themselves:

- Sharing housing due to loss of housing, economic hardship, or a similar reason;
- Living in motels, hotels, trailer parks or camping grounds due to lack of alternative adequate accommodations;
- Living in emergency or transitional shelters;
- Abandoned in hospitals;
- Having a primary nighttime residence that is a public or private place not designed for or ordinarily used as regular sleeping accommodations for human beings;
- Living in cars, parks, public spaces, abandoned buildings, substandard housing, bus or train stations, or similar settings; and,
- Migratory . . . who live in one of the above circumstances. (p. 2)

The Every Student Succeeds Act of 2015 "includes stronger requirements for identifying homeless students," and Blad (2017) identifies guidance for school systems:

- Schools must identify preschool-aged homeless children and ensure that they have access to programs and services they are eligible for, including school-administered preschool programs and the Early Intervention Program for Infants and Toddlers with Disabilities.
- Schools must work to collaborate with other agencies to help meet the needs of homeless students.
- Schools must remove "enrollment barriers, including barriers related to missed application or enrollment deadlines, fines, or fees; records required for enrollment, including immunization or other required health records, proof of residency, or other documentation; or academic records, including documentation for credit transfer." (para. 10)

Homelessness causes educational disruptions for children. According to Ingram, Bridgeland, Reed, and Atwell (2016), "young people have large dreams even in the face of great challenges," and "we learned that to be successful, everyone has a role to play—community leaders, funders, parents, educators, and students" to ameliorate homelessness as a disruption to educational attainment for youth" (p. 1). Homelessness is trauma, and Murphey, Vaughn, and Barry (2013) report that "homelessness is associated with a number of risk factors that may contribute to mental health disorders—such as poverty, family violence and/or dissolution, and school problems—in addition to itself being a potential source of trauma" (p. 2).

Every system needs to have plans on how to support students and parents who face homelessness. Systems can help to break the cycle of homelessness, and as Theoharis (2017) concludes, "Success in life is about the . . . obstacles we overcome . . . , and education is the most valuable asset one can possess on the journey toward gainful employment" (para. 8). Leaders must recognize that homelessness knows no bounds, and nationally there are significant pockets of homeless students and families across urban, suburban, and rural school systems.

Reflecting on the Work

In leading partnerships for shifting communities . . .

1. What conversations about homelessness are occurring in your district?
2. Who within and external to the system have been involved in these conversations?

Health Care

Schools and their systems have access to students for approximately six hours a day, and this puts educators in a position to ensure more healthy children enter the schoolhouse every day, ready to learn. The conversations on health care for children continues with an expanding focus on interagency collaboration. For school programs to support student health and well-being, systems must be ready to build structures, develop policies, and implement practices that extend beyond the confines of the school building and into the community.

Gracy, Fabian, Roncaglione, Savage, and Redlener (2017) urged educators, physicians, service agencies, families, and policy makers to collaborate on behalf of children to mitigate the deleterious effects of the most pronounced health barriers that affect primarily minority and low-income children who attend the most impoverished schools. According to Gracy et al. (2017), common health barriers include asthma, vision and hearing loss, persistent hunger and untreated mental health and behavior problems. School leaders must understand that if children are going to learn then they need to be healthy—24 hours a day.

Recent gains have been made to provide children with health care. Currently, 87 percent of children have health care, with an estimated 42.2 percent having public health insurance coverage and 54.7 percent having private health insurance coverage (Centers for Disease Control and Prevention, 2017). Given programs and resources often available within communities and schools, no child needs to experience health-related barriers to their education.

Enrolling children in health coverage is not just about getting kids health care to fix a decayed tooth or make a visit for strep throat. School systems have the opportunity to change the course of students' lives for those without health care. By leading initiatives that have an impact on students beyond the school day, superintendents take an extra step needed to support children and their success. Educating healthy children is likely the biggest challenge in public education and the most complex, with multiple moving parts in their communities.

Reflecting on the Work

In leading partnerships for supporting the health of children . . .

1. How does your school district respond to the health needs of your students from the inside? And through outside agencies?
2. Have any connections been made in your district between healthy children and achievement?

Nutrition

Over 14 million children live in food-insecure homes in this country, and that number is trending in the wrong direction (Weinfield et al., 2014). Here, both research and simple intuition point to the challenges of teaching students when they are hungry. We know that hungry children just cannot focus on learning. Therefore, superintendents need to take a lead in the charge of ending child hunger by leading the development of programs within and outside the system. Students being hungry at any time poses significant life-and-death health risks that in many ways is even more important than their inability to focus in the classroom.

Federal campaigns have created a national focus on providing healthy meals for all school children. Unfortunately, recent conversations have escalated about the federal hot lunch and breakfast programs regarding healthy food requirements for lunches and the provisions for breakfast programs. We cannot go backwards in the support for healthy meals for all children and superintendents must now jump into the fray.

We understand this growing concern about poor nutrition and its impact on children; yet, have school leaders included these concerns in the conversations to be addressed in planning to improve student performance? Many would predict that until we bring a greater level of resolve to this issue, children in our schools will carry the burden of our lack of attention.

The issue that school leaders often leave off the table is whether students go hungry in the evenings, weekends, and during school vacations. Monday morning class is compromised when students have not had basic meals over the weekend—and do we understand that? Though addressing the total hunger needs of children 24-7 has not typically been a major role of schools, it cannot be marginalized by school leaders. Schools must take a more deliberate role in ensuring that activities with local nonprofit organizations, faith-based organizations, and food banks have ample support to subsidize food for students at home, outside of the school day.

Reflecting on the Work

In leading partnerships for the health and nutrition of students . . .

1. Do students adequately access your district's hot lunch program? What does the data tell you?
2. What conversations are occurring in your community to ensure children do not go hungry?

Student Mobility

Sparks (2016) referred to student mobility as the "churn" and "transience" that signals movement "for reasons other than grade promotion . . . during a school year" (para. 4). Mobility can be "voluntary" as in the case when a student leaves to attend a specialty school or "involuntary" as when a student is expelled for behavioral issues (Sparks, 2016). Typically, when superintendents talk about schools and their performance, the community at large often believes that the student population in their community is stable and that families as a whole do not move. Going one step further, when schools are assessed based on achievement indicators, most people believe that these students have always been enrolled in that school. This is not typically the case in struggling schools.

Nationally, it is not unusual to see a 50 percent student turnover rate in one school over the course of one year. Transiency or student mobility is a major obstacle to student success (Smith, 2011). Impediments to mobility include delayed learning and lower achievement in mathematics and reading (Beaudette, 2014); inability for school systems to be able to focus on student needs because of the "hopscotch" ways in which students move from one system to another or within a system (Welsh, 2016), and countless stressors induced by mobility that can traumatize students.

High mobility rates are also disruptive to non-mobile students "who must deal with the classroom disruption as mobile students enter and exit, and they often experience a slower pace of instruction as new students are incorporated into the class" (Beaudette, 2014, p. 1). Given these impediments and more, superintendents need to look closely at the processes in place to support students who move frequently. When any student walks through their school doors to enroll, the schools must take full responsibility to understand their needs in every way.

When schools take full ownership as soon as students walk through the door, personnel must have effective transition processes in place for every student on the first day of school. Schools need to assess the social, emotional, and academic needs of students. Understanding students' needs from the first day will lead to greater chances of success and less remediation and frustration for the student. When students feel supported and successful quickly, their new learning environment is a place where they can engage and gain confidence.

Reflecting on the Work

In leading partnerships to support students of high mobility . . .

1. How are new students transitioned into your district? At the school level?
2. Are student transitions at the school level personalized or generic?

Mental Health

Do district leaders understand the complexities around mental health? And, are conversations occurring to address mental health or to deal with the aftermath? According to the Report of the Surgeon General's Conference on Children's Mental Health: A National Action Agenda (2000) an estimated 15 million young people can likely be diagnosed with a mental health disorder today. Another staggering statistic is that one half of all lifetime diagnosable mental health conditions begin by the age of 14 (Kessler et al., 2005).

One in five adolescents in this country shows significant symptoms of emotional distress, with nearly 10 percent having symptoms that impair everyday functioning (Knopf, Park, & Mulye, 2008) but that go undiagnosed (Shavers, 2014). Many more students are at risk due to family genetics, issues with families, school, and community, and with interactions with their peers. Moreover, only seven percent of students needing services get them. These statistics are staggering and likely to grow. With this being the condition, schools need to expand their understanding and role in addressing these needs for children. Working with students with mental health issues is not just about developing policies, but rather understanding the issues and developing the proper services and support protocols.

Reflecting on the Work
In leading partnerships for the mental health of students . . . 1. How are mental health services provided in your district? 2. How do you coordinate mental health services in your community to assist students and parents?

Chronic Absenteeism

A chronically absent student is one that misses "at least 15 days of school in a year" and as a result, "are at serious risk of falling behind in school" (U.S. Department of Education, 2013–2014 Civil Rights Data Collection, n.p.). According to the Civil Rights Data Collection (CRDC), chronic absenteeism is a hidden educational crisis, based on the following data:

- Over 6 million students missed 15 or more days of school in 2013–2014—that's 14 percent of the student population—or about 1 in 7 students.
- Chronic absenteeism is about 20 percent less likely among English learners than non-English learners.
- At the high school level, nearly 1 in 5 students are chronically absent— almost 20 percent—whereas 12 percent of students at the middle school are chronically absent; and, almost 11 percent of elementary school students are chronically absent.
- When examining the totality of absenteeism in the United States, approximately 98 million school days are lost per year across K–12. (n.p.)

These data points paint a portrait of the challenges of attendance resulting in students not meeting their educational goals. Attendance needs a sharp focus because, "irregular attendance can be a better predictor of whether students will drop out before graduation than test scores" (CRDC, 2013–2014, n.p.)

For many years, school districts have kept statistics on absenteeism; however, very little has changed in their approaches to deal with this issue. The typical response to students with high absenteeism has been to send a letter after five absences and then after ten absences with the threat of withdrawal from school. One must wonder how this thinking aligns to the work of schools today because it is counterproductive to have this approach if a goal of the district is to educate all children.

Statistics generally look good for schools that often report average attendance rates in the 90 percent range. So, what is the problem? A different story emerges when attendance data are disaggregated because attendance averages may have attendance issues within a segment of their population. In these districts, it is typical to find that some schools have over 20 percent of their students missing over 10 days of school. These numbers should send a strong message—the calculation of absenteeism does not tell you what is needed as a leader.

Leaders have taken a variety of positions on absenteeism ranging from turning the problem solely over to the parents, while others have taken a more punitive approach through policies that have disciplinary consequences. Some districts take away credits for missing school even though students pass the courses. Inherent in this growing problem is a dire need to understand the root cause of the attendance problems at the macro district and individual levels when seeking solutions. This issue will not go away, and the rate of absenteeism will likely grow. The research clearly reflects that high absenteeism impacts student achievement.

District leaders should look at attendance issues through the lens of the conditions that exist today. Such approaches necessitate taking a multipronged approach of support and clarity in seeking solutions. Knoster (2016) offers that school systems should examine their work by employing:

- The effective use of data to identify, monitor, and support the attendance and performance of students at risk of absenteeism.
- Family and community engagement.
- The provision of wraparound services for students facing obstacles to consistent attendance that are outside of school.
- The implementation of social and emotional learning (SEL) supports. (p. 6)

Given the complexities of students' lives, some systems are looking at programmatic offerings that could include, for example, virtual educational options. Given the availability of internet access, even in the most impoverished areas of cities—both urban and rural—the flexibility of online choices can increase student access.

Regardless of the reason for chronic absenteeism, schools must have in place processes to respond at the individual student and family level. No students should be missing school without the attention of school and district personnel. Processes for supporting students' attendance is significant and cannot be minimalized.

Reflecting on the Work
In leading partnerships to ensure student attendance . . . 1. Have you looked at trend data for students absent 5 days, 10 days, and 15 or more days? 2. Do schools have specific initiatives to address attendance issue?

Trauma-Informed Practices

Students come to school traumatized; thus, conversations of late are around the entirety of the challenges and perils all students face every day. Communities and schools are positioned to educate all children when they understand the human trauma children experience in their families, communities, and schools. Today, systems are taking a new approach to address the needs of children and families by implementing trauma-informed practices.

Treatment and Services Adaptation Center (n.d.) extends the thinking about what schools can do to foster safe and inclusive environments:

> In a trauma-informed school, the adults in the school community are prepared to recognize and respond to those who have been impacted by traumatic stress. Those adults include administrators, teachers, staff, parents, and law enforcement. In addition, students are provided with clear expectations and communication strategies to guide them through stressful situations. The goal is to not only provide tools to cope with extreme situations but to create an underlying culture of respect and support. (para. 2)

This means that schools must change to incorporate a "layered approach to create an environment with clear behavior expectations for everyone, open communication, and sensitivity to the feelings and emotions of everyone" (para. 4).

Schools and systems wanting to adopt a trauma-informed approach would adapt the following key elements:

- A whole school approach. A child, in order to feel safe at school, needs to know that they can approach any classroom teacher, specialist, principal, teacher's aide, well-being support, or business manager, and receive the same response. The response needs to be agreed upon by all staff, practiced, and with an accepted process when things don't go the way we hope.
- Assuming complexity, approaching with empathy.

- Commitment to building trust and relationships. We can never stop working on this. For students and families living with prior and ongoing trauma, each day can bring a new struggle, and school can provide a sanctuary.
- Connecting with the whole family.
- Behaviour [sic] as a symptom of the problem, not the problem. This is not to say that violence or breaches of safety do not incur serious consequences, but that the consequences include a depth of investigation and a great deal of support.
- Support children to build the skills that are a struggle for them, and include them in the process.
- Connection with external agencies, because school can't do it all. (Harris, 2017, para. 11)

These approaches suggest that screening begins at the early learning stage in pre-Kindergarten. Partnerships with outside agencies as well as community outreach can help with direct services for children.

Understanding shifting communities has many complexities apart from the school district. However, school districts cannot stop at the school door—they need to engage in every opportunity to support students while at school and outside of the regular day. School districts that understand the impact of trauma on students and their families are better poised to have the right supports in place that will lead to success for all students.

Reflecting on the Work

In leading partnerships for addressing the impact of social trauma . . .

1. Is trauma-informed care part of the district's conversation?
2. How is trauma connected to student well-being and school achievement?

SHARED SPACE AND COLLABORATING
BEYOND THE SYSTEM

Looking back in public education history, it becomes evident that while school districts have developed relationships with organizations and businesses, historically these kinds of relationships were typically peripheral and not central to the organization's success. School districts simply have held a more autonomous approach to their work and did not rely on or tap into the resources of the community. The future success of educating all children will require this approach to change dramatically. These changes will need to be predicated on an innovative approach of sharing space and overlapping resources with organizations outside of the school system.

Business Relationships

For years, schools have been connecting with businesses and manufacturers to create a cadre of workers who are prepared to enter the workforce right out of high school. However, the outcry from business of late is that the workforce does not align to their needs especially in the areas of soft skills (e.g., ability to communicate with coworkers, work in teams, etc.) and not as much in specific skills within the field.

The reemergence of technical programs has spawned programs for students that tap into their interest and the ways they want to learn. It is here that one should consider the concept of "shared space." That is how schools and businesses share space so that there is flexibility between organizations and greater strength in supporting students. In many ways, in the current model, organizations only touch each other with the contact point being students going into the workforce.

A new view is to look at how schools and organizations can work together with a focus on developing and supporting students rather than a single focus of providing only job skills. The goal of the two organizations is to overlap resources with a focus on the whole student who needs support and adult mentoring to help them navigate the perils now associated with being a teenager. In this model, the two systems overlap with shared space for youth development while at the same time engaging students in learning and preparing to be successful in the workforce.

Local Government

The economic vitality of communities is really a function of both government and schools and this goes beyond just creating a viable workforce. Effective and vibrant schools are now in the forefront of most business ventures in decisions to locate their companies. Businesses are critical to the community beyond the economic engine, as many are designed to support their community by improving the conditions for children. Superintendents are crucial members of the economic engine for a community and should see themselves in this role that is beyond the brick and mortar of schools.

Colleges and Universities

Superintendents should not look far for collaborating with colleges and universities that prepare teachers and leaders. Today, schools must have the most effective teachers working with students, and postsecondary institutions need to understand how children learn. School districts and universities need to create new types of relationships with a shared space focusing on the best instructional practices and programs based on research and practice.

No longer can leaders sit back and rely on practice or research alone. Focused and agreed-upon research can bridge the gap between practice and research and thus provides a solid framework for both decision-making, implementation, and assessment of new instructional designs. In today's fast-changing pace, research needs to be current and timely, helping to design instructional practices for the future and not validating past practices.

Community Support Agencies

Most communities, especially those with higher levels of poverty typically have many not-for-profit agencies that have defined social agendas. However, many school districts are not designed to take advantage of these services because they typically occur outside of the school day. Bringing together social agencies to understand each other's roles and defining a joint focus with strong relationships strengthens services for children. New relationships may be found through grants or collaborative projects headed by the district with community agencies. Through such efforts, a range of programs can be developed and maintained while providing continuity of services and minimizing duplication and competition for funds.

Reflecting on the Work

In leading partnerships that share space . . .

1. What relationships and formal partnerships have been developed in your school district with local businesses and manufacturers?
2. How connected is the district to organizations in your community that are, or could be, an asset in educating children?

RISKS IF SYSTEMS REMAIN STATIC

It is quite interesting that public schools have come under great scrutiny about not changing and still reflecting an industrial model that is outdated and archaic. Yet when schools try to change, superintendents come under great fire and often cash in on so much political capital in making structural changes that they need to move on or are directly asked to move on to other employment opportunities. While schools in many ways have changed, the basic structure remains the same and school leaders know this. The challenge is getting communities to support and sustain major shifts in programming curriculum and the overall structure of school.

Knowing your community and how to navigate change as communities shift is a vital element in designing schools that meet all student's needs. Schools need to capture this movement in order to gain footholds that will ensure new programs that support the future landscape take hold. When superintendents take risks by navigating change, they will likely hear statements such as "we have done that before and it does not work" or conversely, "we should put back this program because it worked."

It is important to remember that the metrics for determining what worked or did not work have changed dramatically given different accountability mandates. Secondly, when constituents say that we did this program before and the program was discounted because it did not work as planned back then, the response is, "no we have not specifically done this." The reason why is that when making change, what may be referred to as the third dimension, "time," must be considered. It is not about what goes around comes back around because that only describes the condition in two dimensions. When the third dimension is time, then prior conditions did not exist; therefore, things are not the same.

One of the key concepts to remember when leaders take risks with new programming is that they are likely to be alone, even with strong supporting coalitions. While the intensity about reform and transformation has created much dialogue about changing school structures and processes, most schools will not likely change if the current systems and its metrics work for the majority of the population served. Making change in education is like taking a rubber band and stretching it over an object with a new shape. However, when the rubber band is taken off that object, it snaps back to its original shape.

In many ways, that is what is happening to schools across the country. While we talk about change and transformation, the real result of change is that systems snap back into their original shape. The change is not enduring. Following the rubber band analogy, we cannot afford for our educational system to snap back to the "way it was."

Reflecting on the Work

In leading partnerships to understand the impact of shifting communities . . .

1. What conversations have occurred about the new skill sets needed for students to be successful?
2. What programs have been eliminated or reworked because they no longer prepare students for living and being successful with a new set of conditions?

SUMMARY

Schools and districts cannot remain static, and they must retool to make adjustments if they are going to meet the needs of children in a changing world. Often the cry from within schools is that there are too many initiatives, and schools and systems settle on focusing on one or two at a time. However, superintendents cannot get confused with the "too many initiatives" syndrome while avoiding the emergence of multiple initiatives that support the needs of children in a changing and shifting environment found both within and outside of the system.

Superintendents cannot shy away from continuously developing partnerships, and they must create new systems that develop working relationships with existing and emerging outside organizations. Chapter 4 introduces how superintendents can lead the learning by developing new leaders throughout the system.

A SUPERINTENDENT'S DIVE INTO LEADING IN SHIFTING LANDSCAPES

1. Examine how the current practices in place meet the needs in educating healthy children. How are related "trauma-informed" practices identified in your strategic plan?
2. Review your instructional policies and assess whether they meet the needs of students as they become ready to move forward.
3. Create learning profiles that support the knowledge and skills necessary for students' success in their future. Assess your curriculum in supporting these learner profiles.

SUGGESTED READINGS

Centers for Disease Control and Prevention. (2014). *Health and academic achievement.* Atlanta, GA: Centers for Chronic Disease Control and Prevention.

Frey, W. H. (2014). *Diversity explosion: How new racial demographics are remaking America.* Washington, DC: Brookings Institute.

Gracy, D., Fabian, A., Roncaglione, V., Savage, K., & Redlener, I. (2017). *Health barriers to learning: The prevalence and educational consequences in disadvantaged children.* New York, NY: Children's Health Fund. Retrieved from https://www.childrenshealthfund.org/hbl-literature-review/

Ingram, E. S., Bridgeland, J. M., Reed, B., & Atwell, M. (2016). *Hidden in plain sight: Homeless students in America's public schools.* Washington, DC: America's Promise Alliance. Retrieved from http://gradnation.americaspromise.org/report/ hidden-plain-sight http://nche.ed.gov/briefs.php

Zacarian, D., Alvarez-Ortiz, L., & Haynes, J. (2017). *Teaching to strengths: Supporting students living with trauma, violence, and chronic stress.* Alexandria, VA: Association of Supervision and Curriculum Development.

REFERENCES

Beaudette, P. (2014). *Student mobility in Georgia: Establishing patterns and predictors.* Atlanta, GA: The Governor's Office of Student Achievement.

Blad, E. (2017). ESSA expands schools' obligations to homeless students, new guidance says. *Education Week.* Column is Rules for Engagement: A look at school culture & student well-being. Retrieved from http://blogs.edweek.org/edweek/ rulesforengagement/2016/07/essa_expands_schools_obligations_to_homeless_ students_new_guidance_says.html

Centers for Disease Control and Prevention. (2017). *Health insurance coverage.* Atlanta, GA: U.S. Department of Health & Human Services. Retrieved from https://www.cdc.gov/nchs/fastats/health-insurance.htm

Every Student Succeeds Act. (2015). Pub. L. 114-95, 129 Stat. 1802.

Gracy, D., Fabian, A., Roncaglione, V., Savage, K., & Redlener, I. (2017). *Health barriers to learning: The prevalence and educational consequences in disadvantaged children.* New York, NY: Children's Health Fund. Retrieved from https://www.childrenshealthfund.org/hbl-literature-review/

Harris, R. (2017). Trauma informed practice in action. *Teacher Magazine.* Retrieved from https://www.teachermagazine.com.au/articles/trauma-informed- practice-in-action

Ingram, E. S., Bridgeland, J. M., Reed, B., & Atwell, M. (2016). *Hidden in plain sight: Homeless students in America's public schools.* Washington, DC: America's Promise Alliance. Retrieved from http://gradnation.americaspromise.org/report/ hidden-plain-sight

Kamenetz, A. (2016). As the number of homeless students soars, how schools can serve them better. *nprEd How Learning Happens.* Retrieved from http://www.npr.org/sections/ed/2016/06/13/481279226/ as-the-number-of-homeless-students-soars-how-schools-can-serve-them-better

Kessler, R. C., Berglund, P., Demler, O., Jin, R., Merikangas, K. R., & Walters, E. E. (2005). Lifetime prevalence and age-of-onset distributions of DSM-IV disorders in the national comorbidity survey replication. *Archives of General Psychiatry, 62*(6), 617–627. doi: 10.1001/archpsyc.62.6.617

Knopf, D., Park, M. J., & Mulye, T. P. (2008). *The mental health of adolescents: A national profile.* San Francisco, CA: National Adolescent Health Information Center, University of California, San Francisco.

Knoster, K. C. (2016). *Strategies for addressing student and teacher absenteeism: A literature review.* Washington, DC: U.S. Department of Education, North Central Comprehensive Center.

McKinney-Vento Homeless Assistance Act. (2010). Pub. L. 106–400, 114 Stat. 1675, H.R. 5417 U.S. Department of Education.

Murphey, D., Vaughn, B., & Barry, M. (2013). Access to mental health care. *Child Trends—Adolescent Health Highlight.* Publication # 2013-2. Retrieved from https://www.childtrends.org/wp-content/uploads/2013/04/Child_Trends-2013_01_01_AHH_MHAccessl.pdf

National Center for Homeless Education. (2015). Federal data summary: School years 2011–2012 to 2013–2014. Retrieved from http://www2.ed.gov/programs/homeless/data-comp-sy13-14.pdf

No Child Left Behind Act. (2001). Pub. L. 107-110, 115 Stat. 1425, 20 U.S.C. § 6301.

Shavers, C. A. (2014). Commentary: Emotional problems and depression among children and adolescents in today's society. *Open Journal of Depression,* 74–87. doi: 10.4236/ojd.2014.32012

Sparks, S. D. (2016, August 11). Student mobility: How it affects learning. *Education Week*: Editorial Projects in Educational Research—Issues A–Z. Retrieved from https://www.edweek.org/ew/issues/student-mobility/

Smith, L. (2011). Understanding transiency and how it affects school performance. Smyrna Patch. Retrieved from http://patch.com/georgia/smyrna/bp--understanding-transiency-and-how-it-affects-schoo29673d4c6f

Theoharis, K. (2017). Shelters don't cure homelessness: Here's what can make a difference. *Crain's New York Business.* Op-Ed. Retrieved from http://www.crainsnewyork.com/article/20170224/OPINION/170229991/shelters-dont-cure-homelessness-heres-what-can-make-a-difference

Treatment and Services Adaptation Center. (n.d.). *What is a trauma-informed school?* Retrieved from https://traumaawareschools.org/traumaInSchools

U.S. Department of Education. (2016). *Supporting the success of homeless children and youths: A fact sheet & tips for teachers, principals, school leaders, counselors, and other school staff.* Washington, DC: Department of Education. https://www2.ed.gov/policy/elsec/leg/essa/160315ehcyfactsheet072716.pdf

U.S. Department of Education 2013–2014 Civil Rights Data Collection. (2013–2014). *Chronic absenteeism in the nation's schools: An unprecedented look at a hidden educational crisis.* Retrieved from https://www2.ed.gov/datastory/chronicabsenteeism.html

U.S. Department of Health and Human Services, U.S. Department of Education, U.S. Department of Justice. (2000). Report of the Surgeon General's conference on children's mental health—A national action agenda. Washington, DC: U.S. Department of Health and Human Services. Author. Retrieved from https://www.ncbi.nlm.nih.gov/books/NBK44233/

Weinfield, N. S., Mills, G., Borger, C., Gearing, M., Macaluso, T., Montaquila, J., & Zedlewski, S. (2014). *Hunger in America 2014: National report.* Rockville, MD: Westat and the Urban Institute. Retrieved from http://www.feedingamerica. org/hunger-in-america/our-research/hunger-in-america/

Welsh, R. O. (2016). School hopscotch. A comprehensive review of K-12 student mobility in the United States. *Review of Educational Research, 87*(3), 475–511. doi: 10.3102/0034654316672068

Chapter 4

Leading the Learning

IN THIS CHAPTER . . .

- The Superintendent as the Lead Leader
- Leading the Learning with the Board of Education
- Leading the Learning with District Leaders
- Leading the Learning with Principals
- Leading the Learning with Teachers
- Leading the Learning with Parents and the Community

LETTER FROM THE SUPERINTENDENT

Dear Faculty and Staff:

I am very pleased and humbled by the work of everyone in developing our Commitments for Student Success. The Commitments reflect the collective work that will lead to the success of every student in the district; moreover, they will help us to develop a structure to work differently in preparing our students for opportunities beyond high school. With your help, we are in the process of identifying observable practices and aligning them with the new teacher and leader evaluation processes to ensure that our expectations and definitions are clear.

Along with our Commitments, a new day is unfolding as we prepare to create personalized digital learning environments with a take-home initiative for grades 3–12. State-of-the-art devices do not revolutionize teaching and learning. It is the way we use learning technologies to change instructional practices in innovative ways. This year, for the first time, students will be assigned a Chromebook that they are able to take home, and we have new solutions to ensure all students have internet access.

As we move into exciting times for our students, I look forward to the continued conversation across the district about the needs of our students and the instructional practices that challenge and engage them every day.
Sincerely,
Superintendent

Superintendent leadership in many ways goes well beyond the individual decisions made that affect each level in the system. Leadership may be better assessed by the kind of culture developed through ongoing conversations that occur throughout the organization every day. Leading the right conversations sends a strong message about how the superintendent empowers others to engage and learn, and positions others to assume leadership roles.

Leading by modeling the characteristics of a learner is an attribute that differentiates good superintendents from highly effective superintendents and good districts from dynamic districts. D'Amico (2014) believes modeling is "a moral imperative to continue to learn, stay current and help build capacity throughout the district" (para. 3).

THE SUPERINTENDENT AS THE LEAD LEADER

Leading the learning encompasses the many interactions that superintendents have every day between members of the school and community that affect the culture of the system—if the conversations are predicated on the belief that all children *must* be successful. Inherent in a learning culture is an understanding of the power of trust that is especially critical as systems move through transformations.

The learning culture is at its best when students trust their teachers, parents trust their schools, communities trust their school districts, and when the superintendent is trusted to make good decisions about the district. Superintendents are in their best moment as the lead learner when the right processes, the right engagement, and the right attitudes cultivate the highest levels of trust that support and maintain the changes needed in the system.

Leading the learning will require superintendents to be directly involved in developing leaders who can make "good" decisions at the board level, as teachers in the classroom, as leaders of schools, as administrators at the central office, throughout the support services divisions, and within all facets of the community. The dynamics of this transition will likely result in redefined roles and responsibilities that will yield a more flattened decision-making model. The leaders and decision-making in a flattened system will move from a typical vertical leader structure to one that is horizontal (Zepeda, Lanoue, Creel, & Price, 2016).

As organizations flatten their decision-making structure, decisions are made in collaboration at the closest point of contact that produces better results. That does not mean decision-making is disconnected in the system but rather the flexibility in how decisions are made and by whom are understood and connected to the direction of the district. According to Louis, Leithwood, Wahlstrom, and Anderson (2010), decisions are shared in an organization using a collective leadership framework:

- Collective leadership has a stronger influence on student achievement than individual leadership.
- Almost all people associated with high-performing schools have greater influence on school decisions than is the case with people in low-performing schools.
- Higher-performing schools award greater influence to teacher teams, parents, and students, in particular.
- Principals and district leaders have the most influence on decisions in all schools; however, they do not lose influence as others gain influence.
- School leaders have an impact on student achievement primarily through their influence on teachers' motivation and working conditions; their influence on teachers' knowledge and skills produces much less impact on student achievement. (p. 19)

Although this type of leadership framework can become challenging for superintendents, it does allow for greater responsiveness in making decisions that have long-term impact on the system's ability to improve student performance.

The superintendent must now assume a critical leadership role in 1) sharing decision-making responsibilities, 2) articulating the responsibilities of individuals in the school community, 3) leading the design and implementation of professional development for new and existing leaders, and 4) creating a succession strategy as the mobility of personnel, especially leaders, has a substantive impact on the organization. The complexities of this work will require a new focus on the leadership within the organization. By flattening the decision-making model, core knowledge about instructional leadership becomes the center of the work in developing new leaders.

One of the primary responsibilities superintendents assume today is how they define their work to develop and engage leaders across the system and community. This change in role requires a very different leadership approach. To meet the expectation that all students will be successful, an emerging set of leader qualities and corresponding work looks very different from the qualities and work described in the past. In tomorrow's world, leaders across the system will need to reflect on how they meet the work expectations across the following areas:

1. A culture of risk-taking;
2. All are learners;
3. More than test scores; and,
4. Modeling to set the example for learning.

These four areas serve as the organizers for examining the new work of school community leaders from the superintendent to parent leaders across the system. Leading the learning starts first with the superintendent as detailed in table 4.1.

In a day when the educational landscape is constantly shifting, superintendents who effectively lead both their school and communities will have the best possible outcome given the noise and distractions that exist in

Table 4.1. Superintendent's Leader Qualities and Work for Leading Learning

Leader Qualities	Description of the Work
A Culture of Risk-Taking	• Effective superintendents develop a culture through programming and processes where adult decisions create a system, so all students are successful. • Effective superintendents look to the future for preparing students and designing programs as they take adult risks, so students can go places they never thought they could be.
All Are Learners	• Effective superintendents lead and foster a learning culture where the adults can take risks and stretch their thinking through personalized professional growth. • Effective superintendents see policies as a way to innovate to prepare students for their world. • Effective superintendents employ systems of transparency as well as clarity in leading effective processes to the achievement of district goals.
More Than Test Scores	• Effective superintendents see students as individuals with unique attributes and lead systems where teachers and leaders must know and understand their student's distinctive talents and successes.
Modeling to Set the Example for Learning	• Effective superintendents lead by interacting, modeling, and creating focus conversations on teaching and learning in every aspect of their work. • Effective superintendents require district and school building leaders to work collaboratively in modeling strategies and processes that are essential to improve teaching and learning through their respective roles.

the change process—especially in education. Superintendents, school board members, principals, teachers, and community members cannot do this work alone, but they can do this work collectively if they share the same *space* to meet the needs of students.

This shared space is built on trust, collaboration, and innovation—all with an understanding that the world is changing quickly. In this new day of leading the learning for leaders across the system, superintendents move from a position that all students *can* learn to one where all students *must* learn.

Reflecting on the Work

In leading the learning . . .

1. How would those in your district and community describe you as a learner?
2. Describe the qualities of district leaders in modeling their role as lead learners.

LEADING THE LEARNING WITH THE BOARD OF EDUCATION

When the board and superintendent maintain a healthy and productive relationship with a shared focus on learning, then all students in the school community benefit in unique and special ways. When the relationship between the board and the superintendent becomes a negative focus, reflecting the interest of the board, then the work required to lead the system in supporting student learning is compromised. With this lens, superintendents can get a good read on the focus of the district to make adjustments in their work with the board.

The challenge for superintendents will be the change in conversations and focus for the board as they lead the district. Table 4.2 outlines the qualities and work required from school boards as they emerge as leaders in the district.

A Culture of Risk-Taking

Regardless of the size of the board or its composition, coming together as one is a primary role of the superintendent and the Board President/Chair. With that said, and while it is important to focus on how the board works together, it is equally important to focus on how the board works to create the necessary culture, so students can grow and thrive. While many sitting board members have different perspectives about their work, they ultimately have the key functions of setting *new* directions for the school district in a way that every student is challenged.

Table 4.2. School Board Leader Qualities and Work for Leading Learning

Qualities	Description of the Work
A Culture of Risk-Taking	• Effective school boards commit to a vision of high expectations for student achievement through quality instruction and clearly defined goals that support the district's vision and mission. • Effective school boards have shared beliefs and values about what is possible for all students to learn and of the system's ability to create challenging school experiences every day.
All Are Learners	• Effective school boards align and sustain resources for professional development across the system to meet district goals. • Effective school boards are accountability-driven, spending less time on operational issues and more time focused on policies to improve student achievement. • Effective school boards have a collaborative relationship with staff and the community and establish a strong communications structure to inform and engage both internal and external stakeholders in setting and achieving district goals.
More Than Test Scores	• Effective boards are data savvy. They embrace and monitor multiple pieces of information, even when the information is negative, and they use data to drive continuous improvement.
Modeling to Set the Example for Learning	• Effective school boards lead as a united team with the superintendent, each from their respective roles, with strong collaboration and mutual trust. • Effective school boards take part in team development and training to build shared knowledge, values, and commitments to ensure decisions lead to all students succeeding.

Democracy is the foundation not only for public schools, but also for how our country functions. An elected school board represents the democracy of a community. Their role, which is not much different from most elected officials, is more than a governing board. School boards represent their community constituents and establish processes to ensure that their work is predicated on its values and beliefs. The work of the school board as a collective is to move the needle in supporting and challenging all students. Much of this work is done through establishing the direction for the district through its vision, mission, and beliefs, discussed in chapter 6. Coming together as a board in agreement is not easy given the many views of the community.

First, elected boards have a responsibility to the district, but often feel compelled to make decisions based on the voices of their elected constituency. When board members are elected from different regions of the district, it is important that superintendents lead the board to make decisions for the good of the "whole" community that is best defined by the district's direction rather than the good for "my" voting segment of the district. This aspect of board responsibilities should be a priority in every decision and a marque for effective board governance.

Superintendents must take a lead position with their board to ensure that the vision, mission, and beliefs drive the system, especially amid the push-back often generated on change itself, and even more importantly in decisions to meet the needs of all children. In view of the changing world, the super-intendent and the board will need to take risks with the unknown. More than likely, when schools look to the future for answers to questions on the success of all students, the answers will likely not be found from the past. It has been said that "there soon will be a time when we can no longer predict the future based on the events of the past. For public schools that time has arrived" (Lanoue, 2017a, para. 6).

Decisions to create new systems that look different is likely the most im-portant work of the superintendent and board if the future for educating all students is going to look different. This work becomes especially challenging knowing that designing programs that support students in their world is often an unknown world for many adults. District initiatives to support all students can often be derailed when not everyone is on the same page with the direc-tion of the system.

School systems have an innate tendency to snap back to their traditional state, much like a rubber band snaps back into its original shape. Sustained change can only be initiated and maintained with clarity on what is to be accomplished and how it is going to be accomplished; the two cannot be confused with each other. Too often, adults confuse the "what" with the "how."

All Are Learners

One of the most productive conversations a superintendent and school board can have is about their own learning. When board members or leaders refer-ence their thinking in relationship to some prior experience, it often indicates that they are possibly making decisions using only a historical context and not one based on the future. The board and the superintendent must do their "homework" by looking at critical shifts in how students now learn in the pre-sent to be ready for tomorrow. We must understand the history of programs in relationship to meeting the needs of students for their future worlds. The past gives us some good lessons for how to move forward, but the past will not provide us with the sole answer to how all children can succeed.

The school board and the superintendent should be the most informed collaborative in the school community in understanding the "big" picture for the school district. This will require board members with the leadership from the superintendent to engage in learning opportunities outside of the regular board meetings. While this work may be difficult for board members with other job responsibilities, superintendents should seek ways to provide information in a manner that is easily understood and to create multiple opportunities to discuss trends.

The emerging technology culture opens access doors for school board members in the same way it does for students (see chapter 5). Preparing the board on trends and future innovations can often be on the bottom of the superintendent's list for the work that needs to be done. However, laying the groundwork here will create stability for future discussion and decision-making to create sustained change.

When the board and the superintendent talk about programs in the context of how they can challenge and excite students, that is when they are fulfilling their responsibilities. It is when the board and superintendent get down into the "weeds" that the focus shifts to who makes the decision rather than why the decisions were made. If the board and superintendent model what they expect from students in terms of preparedness with their own learning then more than likely the other adults and students in the system will embrace those qualities as well.

More Than Test Scores

Looking at students holistically has taken a divergent road given the high-stakes nature of accountability. First, accountability is critical to the success of public education and historically, accountability has been woefully inadequate in most schools and districts across the country. The statistics on graduation rates alone, regardless of how these statistics are calculated, has been abysmal, and we must make changes to this issue at the *speed of light*. However, we cannot get so entrenched in test data that many believe is the sole indicator that drives graduation rates, to the extent that we lose sight of our children's needs and how they can be successful.

In the final analysis, students are simply "not data points" because they are much more, and each student's "face contains multiple points of information. It's the stories and the individual circumstances behind each one of these faces that really matter" (Lanoue, 2017b, para. 6). It is incumbent for superintendents and board members to reach out to students. If you just talk with students, you will find out who they are and what they can and want to do. You will not know if they passed the standardized test in all or none of the tested areas. We cannot forget this.

A recent pressure felt by superintendents and school boards is school and district performance based on metrics determined at the state and federal levels that categorize schools as either successful or failing. Our country has developed an increasing social and political infatuation with drawing a single line between failing or succeeding based on a number. Using numerical metrics and data points tells part of the story but not the whole story. Systems will need to determine how to tell the whole story of who our students are and not what they got on the test. To do otherwise creates distortion.

Modeling to Set the Example for Learning

One point to make here is that we all need role models. School boards are often derailed from the core conversations that should be about teaching and learning, mostly because of adult issues. For superintendents and school boards, the most essential element of the collective work is to model the expected behaviors in leading the district. Given that the primary focus of schools is learning, here are some questions to reflect:

- How much of the conversation from the superintendent and school board is about learning, and what does that look like?
- How much of the school board meetings is about instruction or district performance?

Board and school leaders need to set the example and be the role models in the types of conversation and human behaviors that need to occur to create and maintain healthy districts that can grow and change to meet the needs of their students and community. The litmus test for school boards is simply to ask themselves, "Do we want our students to act and engage in problem solving like we do?" One of the largest contradictions in education comes in the form of respectful behavior by school boards around discord on principles, processes, or outcomes.

Uniting school boards and superintendents will not occur without constant energy and professional learning. Regular work sessions on board dynamics is essential to support district planning and making decisions in real time. In many ways, this is like health checkups and making adjustments in one's personal life. If regular checkups do not happen, then issues emerge to the extent, that repair becomes a process that consumes valuable time and energy that the board should be using in leading the district. The issues are often with the adults and not the children.

Reflecting on the Work
In leading the learning with the school board . . . 1. Does your board make decisions based on what is best for their constituents or for the entire district? 2. Have you led your board in developing student and school performance indicators other than state test scores or rankings? What did this process entail?

LEADING THE LEARNING WITH DISTRICT LEADERS

The primary role of district office personnel is to support the work of the superintendent. The first questions for the superintendent to ask are, 1) what is our role in the district, and 2) how does this role provide support throughout the system? Too often, central office personnel are seen as barriers to the work needing to be accomplished at the school level. The secondary role of district office staff is to support the efforts that directly and indirectly affect the work in schools.

The district office should not be seen as an entity in and of itself. Often, central office staff are seen as creating more work for schools. Moreover, school leaders believe they are merely completing work assigned originally to central office staff. In the final analysis, district office staff are a direct reflection of the superintendent; therefore, they have a significant role and responsibility in leading ways that are supportive of achieving short- and long-term goals of the system.

New programs should always be tested first and then used by district office personnel as appropriate. The adults in schools and the community need to see that district leaders are working to have the skills in areas to support them. As an example, if new technology is introduced, then central office personnel need to be the first to convert to new systems. Modeling by district office leaders may be the most powerful practice for the system's effectiveness.

Superintendents set the expectations of the district office by what they say and what they do. If superintendents *"believe it then they need to lead it"* (Zepeda & Lanoue, 2017, p. 61, emphasis in the original). What superintendents believe is important must transcend through the entire system. As much attention in developing leaders that support the direction of the schools should also be given to principals, teachers, and community members.

Reflecting on the Work
In leading the learning with the district team . . . 1. How do you align the work of district divisions to support the success of strategic plan initiatives? 2. What conversations provide evidence that your district team has the expertise to carry out their roles?

LEADING THE LEARNING WITH PRINCIPALS

Superintendents establish themselves as the lead leader of the school district only if they have a direct impact on the work of school principals. Principals can no longer be the "manager" or the ones who maintain "law and order." If school leaders see their role as maintaining order and compliance then we essentially fail our primary responsibility—done and end of story. However, if we want vibrant schools that have a direct focus on learning throughout the system, then superintendents need to lead a contemporary set of expectations for school leaders and must lead by what they do, by what they say, and by how they view work, as elaborated in table 4.3.

While superintendents have many priorities, working with school leaders cannot be delegated or left to chance because we know from a robust research base that principals are second only to teachers in improving both teacher quality and student learning (Darling-Hammond, 2007; Hallinger, 2011).

A Culture of Risk-Taking

The first questions in any school should be about the unique needs of the students they serve. Central questions about the school's programs and processes to support students should drive the conversation between the superintendent, district leaders, and school principals. Although these questions at first blush appear straightforward, they are only the door into a system involving complex processes and changes in adult and student behaviors.

Preparing principals to reshape an often static structure where students are stuck "in their lanes" requires intense focus by the superintendent coupled with deliberate professional engagement activities that reshape principals' skill sets with a vision to lead a new learning culture (Zepeda, Jimenez, & Lanoue, 2015). Working with principals to develop their leader skills and knowledge is the fulcrum of the system; the system can go either way—a

Table 4.3. Principal Leader Qualities and Work for Leading Learning

Qualities	Description of the Work
A Culture of Risk-Taking	• Effective principals include teachers and support personnel in designing and implementing innovative practices aligned to the district strategic plan. • Effective principals develop processes to ensure students can take academic risks with their own learning with the supports needed to be successful.
All Are Learners	• Effective principals leverage human capital, leading collaborative planning models with teachers to promote growth—individually and collectively. • Effective principals foster a culture where teachers can innovate in a safe and supportive setting. • Effective principals are visible leaders who engage with and monitor programs and processes needed for all students to learn and grow.
More Than Test Scores	• Effective principals have systems in place where every student is viewed as having unique individual talents that are known and developed. • Effective principals view students as individuals and not as data points.
Modeling to Set the Example for Learning	• Effective principals develop teacher leaders who are resources for their colleagues. • Effective principals create opportunities for teachers to grow and assume responsibility for their own professional learning in support of the district's direction.

system where some students are successful *or* a system where all students are successful.

To prepare principals in shaping a new school culture where the adults take risks with their own thinking about students goes well beyond monthly meetings. Preparing principals requires risk-taking by the superintendent as well as pervasive conversations about the work needed at the school level. Preparing principals to do this work does not occur without the superintendent creating purposeful and deliberate processes to get them ready.

Regardless of the size of the school system, superintendents cannot be passive observers in the leader development process. Superintendents must be at the front and center in the development, content, and delivery of principal development processes. Through this involvement, superintendents are seen as champions for effective leadership and school transformation to ensure the success of all students. To do the same work we have been doing and making the same decisions on only what is believed to work historically will not change the experience for students in a way we need now.

If what worked in the past worked for all students, then we would not be in the position we are in today. Today requires a new thinking where all students will learn regardless of their experiences outside of school. Creating a culture where innovation and change becomes the trademark requires a shift in thinking from traditional school improvement teams. Desai (2017) describes the characteristics of innovative teams as having 1) realistic expectations, 2) credibility among their peers, 3) strong processes, 4) a well-rounded composition, and 5) integration into the organization. In addition, Desai (2017) points out that these teams can only be successful when the leader has patience, collaborative skills, and a vision.

The same expectations hold true for students in that adults need to take risks. It is appalling when you hear someone say, "I knew when she was in third grade that she would probably not graduate." The question is, "what did you or the school do when the child was in third grade?" Keeping students in their lanes is a total contradiction to what schools work to achieve. School leaders need to lead a culture where they change what students see for themselves and not what the adults only see in them. We need to determine how systems take risks, especially with shifting communities (see chapter 3).

All Are Learners

The work of the superintendent in developing principals as lead learners can easily be determined by examining principal meeting agendas, how school visits are conducted—if at all—and what conversations are occurring during leader reviews or school performance reviews. Two questions to ask include:

1. How much of the agenda is focused squarely on innovation and practices that support the learning needs of students?
2. How is that supported at the school and district levels?

In every way, the new leader is the new learner only if it starts at the top and adds meaning to the system. However, developing learners is not about book studies, going to conferences, or participating in webinars; rather, the work is about how leaders take in new information and use it to lead innovation and change in their buildings on behalf of students and the adults who teach them.

Systems today often give the appearance of being learning systems, but is this just a "new veneer top" on an old cabinet? Often, little has changed when one looks deeply into the system's beliefs and practices. The world of education has created too many situations where leaders espouse practices and ask others to do work that they themselves do not fully understand. The adage that "one is dangerous with a little information" may pique interest, but it will not go deep into influencing the system unless the processes are fully understood by its leaders.

When superintendents visit schools, what do they do?

- Do they stop in at the main office, chat with the principal, stroll the halls, and then leave?
- Alternatively, do they walk classrooms with the principal to discuss instructional practice as it relates to planning, delivery, and results?

Walks with principals to engage in these kinds of conversations about instruction models the expectations of the system leader (Zepeda & Lanoue, 2017). School visits are more than operational or crisis-driven; they provide professional learning conversations for leaders about clarity and depth of effective practices.

Assessing the "learning principal" may be best captured by asking those in the building a question, "who leads and drives the learning?" Responses such as lead teachers and so-called curricular specialists may provide insight into the role of the principal as a learner. If the principal is not mentioned as one of the lead learners in the building, then a closer look may reveal effectiveness. Principals best assume their primary responsibility of fostering a learning culture when they themselves are required to be engaged in their own learning.

More Than Test Scores

Understanding and articulating the role of test scores may be the most difficult challenge for school boards, superintendents, and principals to navigate. The heavy reliance and often inaccurate and inappropriate use of testing as the primary factor in the performance of students, teachers, and schools is simply out of balance. For the sake of accountability, testing schemes and other assessment frameworks are one critical element in the overall improvement efforts of schools—but these metrics do not tell the full story. Unfortunately, the pressure in the end lies directly on the students who now see their test scores having a heavy hand in the evaluation of schools, districts, teachers, and principals.

In the days of overtesting, principals were always asked to put a face to every data point. Why? It is important that every day you are reminded of why every student needs to be challenged and supported. Today, we should look at our students much differently. Now, we should understand that every face has personal information behind it that gives insight about who they are and what they need (Lanoue, 2017b). The challenge for principals comes in framing a new accountability system with the district and community that is based on the unique attributes of every student.

Modeling to Set the Example for Learning

At the building level, principals who engage in their own professional learning set the tone for faculty and staff to do the same. Identifying potential leaders and developing their skills is one of their primary responsibilities. While in the current climate of school accountability, not all teachers or staff necessarily want to be a principal or administrator; however, leader opportunities can be developed with a less hierarchical decision-making structure within the organization. When schools create horizontal decision-making models, teachers and staff can then assume leadership roles, affording them opportunities to make decisions within the scope of their work responsibilities.

When superintendents stop and forecast how leadership would change in their organization over three to five years, it will become glaringly obvious that a leader succession plan needs to be in place. Developing new leaders within the system and seeking leaders from outside the system requires a balance that is directly related to the needs and gaps in the system. New perspectives combined with in-house thinking can provide a level of new thinking and the continuity required for effective change processes.

Reflecting on the Work

In leading the learning with principals . . .

1. How do you see your role in developing and monitoring the work of principals?
2. What criteria do you use to know if principals are instructional leaders?

LEADING THE LEARNING WITH TEACHERS

In many school districts, the role of the superintendent may be seen as far removed from teachers and their work in classrooms. Obviously, the size of a district has a significant impact on time and the direct role superintendents can sustain in the context of all of their responsibilities. Teachers need to see and believe that the superintendent understands and is readily engaged in the work that they do every day. It does not necessarily mean that the superintendent can be in classrooms every day, but it does require the superintendent to create opportunities to visit schools and classrooms.

Table 4.4. Teacher Leader Qualities and Work for Leading Learning

Qualities	Descriptions of the Work
A Culture of Risk-Taking	• Effective teachers see opportunities for all children. • Effective teachers encourage and support students to stretch their understanding of who they are and what they can do.
All Are Learners	• Effective teachers embrace the concept of learner agency and allow students to explore the use of multiple resources and learning modalities. • Effective teachers are passionate about what they teach and instill this passion in their students while allowing them to grow in different ways. • Effective teachers communicate their strengths as teachers when they are successful at challenging all students.
More Than Test Scores	• Effective teachers see students for who they are and not just for what they know.
Modeling to Set the Example for Learning	• Effective teachers see all students as having leadership qualities and establish opportunities for them to grow. • Effective teachers use multiple strategies to enrich learning for every student. • Effective teachers are lifelong learners and they engage in myriad forms of job-embedded learning as part of their work with students and colleagues.

We know that the greatest impact on student learning occurs in the classroom as a direct result of the work of teachers, and this is the reason why superintendents need to have a significant instructional focus. Teachers know when superintendents are removed from their work and when the responsibility of instructional leadership is delegated to someone else. To support an instructional culture, superintendents need to find the time and have confidence in themselves to have conversations about instructional practices.

Table 4.4 describes the qualities and work required of teachers in leading classroom designs where all students are successful.

A Culture of Risk-Taking

Does the superintendent remain complacent in her/his approach to learning? Do they push the envelope and initiate conversations that lead to changes in policies, programs, and a culture that allows teachers to take risk with their practices to challenge students? The superintendent is positioned to take risks that positively affects students when the decisions are based on the needs of students and not the needs of adults.

Risk-taking for teachers needs to be fostered through trust and the willingness of the system to allow them to be creative and innovative; however, inherent in risk-taking must be a belief in taking students to new places. Superintendents will need to change their focus from maintaining and leading the current system to creating and leading new systems (Zepeda et al., 2016).

Superintendents send many messages about their district. Sending a message to challenge students becomes a strong signal for teachers to develop new learning cultures in their classrooms. Several questions for teachers to ask themselves as they look at their class for the first time at the beginning of the year illustrates this point.

1. Who do I see?
2. What aspirations do I have for them?
3. Does it differ because of what I know about them or their family, whether they come from poverty, the color of their skin, the language they speak or the parents they have or do not have?
4. What do they see for themselves?

We ask students to take risks and challenge themselves; yet, we often impose many barriers that range from tracking systems to sorting prerequisites. These barriers limit students. Taking risks is not only about shifting beliefs about students but also about taking risks in changing adult practices that do not work for all students.

All Are Learners

Most district vision and mission statements forward that the work in the classroom is to engender in students a passion for learning and for them to become lifelong learners. The question to ask is, "what's more important, what we say or what we say and do?" In a time of exponential change in the world around us, our teachers must design lessons to engage all students in multiple ways. Schools can no longer tolerate the old lesson plans and the activities that were designed to teach all kids in the same ways. To make this shift, teachers will be required to model for themselves that lifelong learning and accessing new information is a necessity. Dynamic teaching will only emerge from those that engage in their own learning, and this quality needs to be recognized and supported in the system.

Superintendents will need to be prepared to engage teachers in conversations that allow them to create opportunities to meet students' interests and learning modalities. The instructional framework of "stand and deliver" no longer has its place if teachers are going to develop lifelong excitement for learning. We can no longer turn off the student switch for their passions.

More Than Test Scores

With high-stakes accountability, the pressure on teachers to have students perform well on standardized test has become both intense and immense. The pressure to have students score well on tests has changed the culture for many schools. This pressure has changed how teachers and school leaders approach their work. While this focus on all students reaching higher levels has made some positive changes in public education, the practices to impact performance of students in various subgroups remains marginalized.

The dangers of the current accountability systems have been a pendulum swinging too far into the belief that "everything" must be quantifiable, with an overarching reliance on high-stakes testing results. In this time of intense accountability, "where is the balance?" In a high-stakes world, the mantra has been that every data point had a face. The issue here is that the score on a test does not tell the story. The entirety of interactions that occur between teachers and their students cannot be distilled into a number. The pattern of teaching to the test must be redirected and not be confused with teachers using high-impact learning standards that challenge students in very different ways.

Superintendents play a critical role in creating and articulating that balance, not only for teachers but also for school leaders and their communities. The major gains in school performance occur when teachers understand who students are as much as what they know about their subject matter.

Modeling to Set the Example for Learning

Teaching requires the use of complex thinking to design strategies so that all students are challenged. No more can the adults say that a student exceeded his or her expectations because that sets the bar too low. Teachers must create lessons for the whole group by understanding the individual needs of every student. Teachers can no longer hold students back and keep them in tracks to their future—isn't teaching about expansion of thinking?

Designing challenging lessons for every student requires an understanding of the individuality of students in order to evoke their engagement, joy, and confidence. Creating a culture where the adults model learning will require a shift in beliefs about teaching everyone in the same way to one where new classroom and school practices support and engage all students as individuals. A starting point should be that every student is an engaged learner who has innate passions. Teaching is about inquiry, trial and error, success and regroup, and having a choice to explore the world. Learning is about the individual meaning of life and not about the book or test. Learning is about what is taken away and applied both in thought and in action. Teachers must model this kind of learning. All students grow in an environment where interest and curiosity are used to build skills and critical thoughts.

Teachers must model for students their own excitement for learning. This excitement becomes the fabric of who they are as a teacher. Students will grow only when teachers grow. Students are keenly aware of teachers who see their work as finite and those who are engaged because of their love of learning. Learning is not finite, nor does it end with a unit test or final exam. It is here where teachers and leaders can shift education to a place that sets the example for the love and need to access lifelong learning. Lifelong learning and reaching new heights will only be the priority when the adults make it so in their own work.

Reflecting on the Work

In leading the learning for teachers . . .

1. In your voice as the superintendent, what do you say about teachers? About specifics of their craft?
2. How do you describe the work in the classroom as leading to the success of all students?

LEADING THE LEARNING WITH PARENTS AND THE COMMUNITY

The significance of communities in the success of schools has changed drastically with the increasing community role in charter schools, vouchers, and school choice as well as the emergence of community school models. These changes often have stimulated a new sense of needed ownership of schools by their communities. The central questions for community members center on the metrics used to determine good schools. However, in reflection we must ask "good schools for who?" and "what is the role of schools in their community?"

During many reform movements, schools remain the foundation for our country and must remain the foundation in our communities. Schools are more likely to meet the needs of all children when communities are supportive and understand the educational framework from which the district and its schools function. What remains critical is that communities with schools that struggle must be engaged in order to improve them. The shifting

Table 4.5.   Responsive Community Leader Qualities and Work for Leading Learning

Qualities	Description of the Work
A Culture of Risk-Taking	• Engaged community members embrace the need to challenge every student, so they have choice once they graduate from high school. • Engaged community members believe that they have a responsibility for youth development so students can navigate social perils.
All Are Learners	• Engaged community members are involved in student activities outside of the school day to activate their curiosity. • Engaged community members get involved in their school to share their knowledge and wisdom. • Engaged community members support their schools and access community assets to support every student.
More Than Test Scores	• Engaged community members see the potential in every child.
Modeling to Set the Example for Learning	• Effective community members engage through modeling expected behaviors as adults. • Effective community members engage with their school system and understand that educating all children needs to be the epicenter of their community.

role of community leaders in supporting children must be understood by superintendents.

It has often been said in many communities that children will "get a good education in our schools if they want one." This position needs to shift to one that says you are going to "get a good education regardless of the circumstances." The role of communities in educating students remains paramount in moving to a place where all students are successful in schools. Healthy communities generate healthy schools, and healthy schools create healthy communities. Table 4.5 lists the qualities that are emerging in community leaders as schools and their communities come together as one.

A Culture of Risk-Taking

Communities easily attach value to their schools based on test scores or state and federal ratings often with very little knowledge about their schools, its challenges or successes, and most of all, its students. Superintendents have a critical role in bringing communities together in ways to understand the needs of their schools. When members of the community support their schools, students feel valued.

Community support starts with setting the high bar for all students that goes well beyond graduation rates. Graduation rates are of great concern— but not an end. Moreover, it is not always about some going to college and some going directly into the workforce. It is about the expectations that students have choices once they graduate.

Having real choices after graduation becomes the greatest hurdle for students who struggle in school. It is here that community members' active role can change the trajectory for students. However, just saying that students can be successful and have choices is easy to do, but implementing practices that support these beliefs is where school and communities normally fall short. Overall, school and school districts do not have systems in place to overlap with resources in their communities.

Often members of the community think that most experience school in the same way that they did which can be positive or negative. Many in communities fail to understand that the challenges students face today are different— we are in a very different day. It was said that students moving through their school years is like crossing a footbridge over a very deep canyon. Communities provide the railings for students when they make mistakes or poor choices—all typically part of the learning process. Therefore, when students make bad choices, the railing catches them.

Without railings, students go into a free fall that is difficult for them to recover from. Families that are transient and live in isolation have few supports or limited railings for their children when they need help. Additionally, the adults are in such crisis that they themselves cannot be the railings for their children especially when alone in isolation. This is where communities need to stand up and not tear down. This is where communities need to support struggling students and struggling schools. The adults and the collective assets of the community need to come together as one for all children, especially those most at risk. Community schools are at their best when each member of the school community is a strong advocate for all children, even if they do not know them.

All Are Learners and Modeling to Set the Example for Learning

While schools and districts debate the equity in resources across schools, often communities fail to realize that the needs of children are not equitable and assets from their homes and communities are not always equitable. A simple example illustrates this point. Some schools will tout very high Advanced Placement (AP) scores while other schools have mediocre AP scores. Is this a school issue, or a curricular or instructional problem? Would you draw the same conclusion if you knew that over 50 percent of the students from the school with high AP scores had tutors for ten hours a week while the other school had none? This example illustrates the important point that outside resources make a significant difference in the success of students and their communities.

Expanding efforts to create greater equity in each school community to engage students opens new doors and opportunities for schools to access needed outside resources. Working with community leaders to unleash human assets that are never tapped can bring new energy and expertise into the schools. However, members of the community are more likely to get involved if the school has structures for them to engage in important work. Determining how the community can help in schools should be the first step for superintendents in leading the learning for their communities.

When schools are at the center of their communities, they have a unique opportunity to create identity with the culture of its community. Students need to believe that the adults in their community are valuable resources. Finally, we can no longer allow the adults in our community to say, "do as I say and not as I do." Superintendents can send a strong message about the value of community by what they say, do, and the actions to reach out to them in support of children. Whether it is through policy or community partnerships and grants, superintendents need to break new ground because if they do not, likely no one will.

More Than Test Scores

Superintendents are often in a difficult situation as they traverse their beliefs about the individual needs of students and how needs are supported in schools. Student achievement, especially as measured by multiple indicators, must remain a priority, but only a priority in the context of each individual student. Working with the community to understand its schools, students, teachers, and leaders is crucial for the complexities of schooling to be understood and to broaden the conversation beyond only test scores.

The key to this shift reverts to the mission, vision, beliefs, and strategic plans of the district. If the direction of the district is simply to increase test scores and has a narrow focus on defining student success this way, then the conversation will remain narrow and limiting. Schools that are able to identify and celebrate the many successes of *all* students in all areas of their school and community position themselves to have conversation to move beyond a test score and to a place where the potential of all students is realized.

Without this focus by superintendents and direction of the district, students will continually be marginalized by those in the school and in the community resulting in a failure to see every child's good and every child's potential. If the school and its community does not see potential in all students, then who will?

Reflecting on the Work
In leading the learning for parents . . . 1. Have you developed a community-wide understanding of what student success looks like in your district? 2. How have you navigated the challenges for groups of students when you know they are struggling in their schools and parents question them being there?

SUMMARY

Superintendents who position themselves to develop effective leaders across the system develop cultures where ownership and decision-making forms the fabric of a system—a system that can take risks and make changes in response to emerging needs. This shift in leadership patterns will only occur when superintendents understand the value in establishing school and community leadership opportunities.

The decision with the most significant impact on education, and one requiring risk-taking, will be the decision to transform schools given the exponential growth of technology and the needs for students to have access to information around the globe. Chapter 5 outlines the importance of student access, and the significance of the expanding digital landscape.

A SUPERINTENDENT'S DIVE INTO LEADING THE LEARNING

1. Engage in a school board self-assessment process or review a self-assessment that has been completed. Use this information to design professional learning to support growth by members of the school board to strengthen their roles for leading and modeling the attributes of the district.
2. Review and revise district and building leader job descriptions to ensure they have a defined responsibility to be the leaders of learning.
3. Examine district and school structures in place for community engagement and revise if necessary to take full advantage of the assets in the community and its leaders.

SUGGESTED READINGS

Purinton, T., & Azcoitia, C. (Eds.). (2016). *Creating engagement between schools and their communities: Lessons from educational leaders.* Lanham, MD: Rowman & Littlefield.

Tschannen-Moran, M., & Tschannen-Moran, B. (2017). *Evoking greatness: Coaching to bring out the best in educational leaders.* Thousand Oaks, CA: Corwin Press.

Van Deuren, A. E., Evert, T. F., & Lang, B. A. (Eds.). (2015). *The board and superintendent handbook: Current issues and resources.* Lanham, MD: Rowman & Littlefield.

REFERENCES

D'Amico, T. (2014, January 13). *Learning and leading in the 21st century: 10 tips by an administrator for administrators.* [Blog post]. Retrieved from http://edblog. smarttech.com/2014/01/learning-and-leading-in-the-21st-century-10-tips-by-an-administrator-for-administrators/

Darling-Hammond, L. (2007). Excellent teachers deserve excellent leaders. In *Education leadership: A bridge to school reform.* New York, NY: The Wallace Foundation. Retrieved from www.wallacefoundation.org/knowledge-center/school-leadership/key-research/Pages/Bridge-to-School- Reform.aspx

Desai, A. (2017, July 21). Successful innovation teams share these 5 realistic traits. *CMO by Adobe.* Retrieved from http://www.cmo.com/opinion/articles/2017/7/7/the-5-elements-of-successful-innovation-teams.html#gs.IctnkzA

Hallinger, P. (2011). Leadership for learning: Lessons from 40 years of empirical research. *Journal of Educational Administration, 49*(2), 125–142. doi:10.1108/09578231111116699

Lanoue, P. D. (2017a, August 1). Why our schools need to lead for tomorrow, not for today. [Blog]. *Course Correction. TrustED.* Retrieved from http://trustedk12.com/course-correction-school-leadership/

Lanoue, P. D. (2017b, September 5). To create a learner-centric culture, understand the story behind every face. [Blog]. *Course Correction. TrustED.* Retrieved from http://trustedk12.com/course-correction-learner-centric-school-leadership/

Louis, K. S., Leithwood, K., Wahlstrom, K. L., & Anderson, S. E. (2010). Investigating the links to improved student learning: Final report of research findings. New York, NY: The Wallace Foundation. Retrieved from www.wallacefoundation.org

Zepeda, S. J., Jimenez, A. M., & Lanoue, P. D. (2015). New practices for a new day: Principal professional development to support learning cultures in schools. *LEARNing Landscapes, 9*(1), 303–319. ISSN 1913-5688

Zepeda, S. J., & Lanoue, P. D. (2017). Conversation walks: Improving instructional leadership. *Educational Leadership, 74*(8), 58–61. Retrieved from http://www.ascd.org/Default.aspx

Zepeda, S. J., Lanoue, P. D., Creel, W. G., & Price, N. F. (2016). Supervising and evaluating principals—The new work of superintendents and central office personnel. In J. Glanz & S. J. Zepeda (Eds.), *Supervision: New perspectives for theory and practice* (pp. 63–79). Lanham, MD: Rowman & Littlefield.

Chapter 5

Leading in a World of Access

IN THIS CHAPTER . . .

- The New Student Learner
- What We Know Today About Tomorrow
- Why Access Is Important
- The Risks in Planning for Tomorrow

LETTER FROM THE SUPERINTENDENT

Dear High School Students:

On many occasions, I have heard you ask the question, "why do I have to attend high school for four years? . . . I have specific plans and can do the work in less time which would allow me to move on with a diploma." I am pleased to let you know that we have a possible solution. You now have new options to enroll in a postsecondary program either full- or part-time starting at ninth grade. You can participate fully in high school activities; yes, you will receive your high school diploma; and yes, you will walk across the stage at the graduation ceremony.

Thanks to our legislators, a new law entitled Move On When Ready (MOWR) that is a revised dual enrollment program allows high school students (ninth through twelfth grade) to earn college credit while working on their high school diploma. The amazing aspect of this option is that it will not cost you for tuition or expenses because the MOWR program now covers tuition, mandatory fees, and required textbooks.

The new MOWR program is easier for you to understand as compared to previous dual enrollment programs. The goals of MOWR are to increase college access and completion and to prepare you to enter the workforce with the skills you need to succeed. Once again, this is an incredible opportunity for all of our students. Please talk with your parents and counselors to understand how this program supports your goals.

As always, thank you for your hard work and dedication to your studies. Sincerely,
Superintendent

Designing schools to meet the needs of all children will require a complete redesign of how schools operate today; however, the transformation process will not be an easy or a quick undertaking. With fast-changing career paths and emerging workplace requirements, schools cannot wait for the workplace to take the lead in defining needed skills. Schools will need to have a more deliberate focus on the skills needed for students to be successful by working with the business and postsecondary education sectors in the development of programs to prepare students to engage in new work. In this fast-paced world, schools must be nimble, responsive, and ready to make changes based as much on prediction as on historical data.

The emergence of technology will continue to change the face of who we are and how we live. Internet access opens the doors to a view of the world never seen before, and schools must be able to embrace the digital world for a rapidly changing future. Learning can no longer be insular as technology provides learning opportunities beyond the school walls.

The complexities of bringing different perspectives on school programs that emerge from rapidly changing career skills, multiple cultures and languages spoken, poverty, and social trauma will require very difficult conversations to produce the results needed. The ability for all students and all families to agree on how they can collectively achieve equal access to what each student needs, especially through a change process, may be the most important challenge for every educational leader.

Superintendents will need to engage in direct conversations about how this new world changes the many traditional staples that are currently the foundation for how schools operate today. These conversations must be about drastically reshaping educational opportunities, so students can engage in their own learning to be prepared as the work skills change around them.

THE NEW STUDENT LEARNER

While the use of learning styles and learning attributes to differentiate instruction has been around for some time, the context for the new learner starts first with identifying the skills and knowledge that students need to be

Table 5.1. New Skills for Students

Core Skills	Brief Description
1. Love of Learning	Learning is challenging, interesting, rewarding, and fun.
2. Skill at Learning	Reflecting and acting on how they learn.
3. Self-Knowledge	Listening and learning.
4. People Sense	Collaborating with strong people skills.
5. Communication	Speaking and writing skills.
6. Worldliness	Not judging the world of others.
7. Comfort with Complexity	Understanding complex issues not easy to solve.
8. Goal Setting	Developing and meeting personal goals.
9. Open Minds	Being able to adapt and change.

Adapted from Mahaffie (2017)

successful in their world. Schools across our country who have emerged as leaders in new school design begin by first understanding the dynamics of learning that will have a positive impact for students on what they need for tomorrow, not yesterday.

Schools that initiate new learning constructs are designed so that learning experiences are founded on a different teaching and learning framework rather than building on and reshaping the traditional one. Unfortunately, many school reform efforts remain predicated on traditional constructs.

New Skills

Should we do the same work to support student's acquisition of skills? Mahaffie (2017) identifies nine core skills that are very different from the skills we talk about in schools today. For students to be future ready, education will need to support students in acquiring skills to be ready for their world. Table 5.1 examines these skills.

These skills paint a very different picture of what we do today. Continuing to develop obsolete skills serves no purpose except to exacerbate and continues the current disconnect in schools today. Making a shift to support a different set of skills is not an easy one because it cuts against the grain of many current constructs (college entrance requirements, entry level jobs, federal and state laws and regulations, etc.) that greatly influence educational practice.

The controversy created by high-stakes testing and Common Core State Standards has limited the ability for schools to support the skills needed for students' future success. The traditional content knowledge that has for so long driven educational practice will need to shift to more process-oriented skills. To move forward, schools will need to define, with both clarity and a level of ambiguity within a fast-changing world, the skills students need to be successful.

New Questions

The skills needed for students to be successful requires educational leaders to ask very different questions about the design of schools. Students need to develop competency in process-related skills rather than knowledge of solely curricular content. Lanoue (2017) discusses the questions that need to be asked, using the Nellie Mae Education Foundation's (*Student Centered Approaches*, n.d.) four pillars of an individualized and learner-centric culture:

- **Learning Is Personalized:** In your classrooms, do students engage in their learning in different ways and in different spaces? Do they benefit from individualized work and formative assessments meant to address students' needs and interests?
- **Learning Is Competency-Based:** Can students move ahead on a subject when they have demonstrated mastery of content as opposed to when they have undergone the required hours in a classroom?
- **Learning Happens Anytime, Anywhere:** Does learning take place beyond the traditional school day or the school year? Or, is it restricted to the classroom?
- **Students Take Ownership Over Their Learning:** Are students engaged in their own success? Are their personal and academic interests incorporated into the learning process? (para. 10, emphasis in the original)

No longer can the questions be about schedules and the routines defined by blocks, semesters, or the length of a learning period. The focus and questions about school practices should be squarely directed toward how to build the capacity of students to be learners. We are no longer in the industrial age where the assembly line stops with a test at the end of the year. The world of access allows for the creation of new models that are adaptable to the needs and potential of each student (Education Reimagined, 2015).

New Learners

The new learners are very different. They want to construct their learning experiences around who they are, and what excites them. Their learning is more relevant to who they are, their families, cultures, and heritage. They want to join others who have their same passions and want to see that their work makes a difference. Opening these opportunities requires students to have choices.

Many teachers across the country attempt to help students make sense about their learning to activate interest and to stimulate curiosity through choices. However, these kinds of opportunities for students remain limited due to the rigidity inherent in a traditional culture. Often choice and interests are relegated to minor changes in the classroom with little impact on the traditional approach characterized in the current one–size-fits-all model.

New learners see beyond their school, community, state, and country; they see the world. We need to understand that all students require the abilities to understand how they learn and to engage in their learning. According to New Learning (n.d.), students will need to see themselves very differently. The new learner:

- Is actively and purposefully engaged in their learning; the most effective learning is engaged learning.
- Belongs in their learning, connecting their identity, subjectivity, and agency into their learning.
- Brings their experience, interests, and voice to the learning task at hand.
- Takes responsibility for their learning through a measure of autonomy and self-control.
- Is a knowledge producer, drawing upon a range of available knowledge resources.
- Works effectively in pairs or groups on collaborative knowledge projects, and creates knowledge to be shared with peers.
- Continues to learn beyond the classroom, using social media to learn anywhere and anytime—the phenomenon of ubiquitous learning.
- Is comfortable in multimodal, digital knowledge creation spaces, bringing together text, image, diagram, video, sound, dataset, instant messaging, etc.
- Critically self-assesses and reflects upon their learning.
- Uses and gives feedback in "social networking" interactions, learning in recursive feedback loops involving peers, parents, experts, and invited critical friends—as well as teachers.
- Engages in intensive horizontal communications and collaborative learning.
- Is a comfortable player in environments where intelligence is collective— not just the sum of things that can be retained in the individual's head, but a capacity to source specialised [sic] knowledge from experts or group members, to negotiate and synthesise [sic] knowledge in groups and to search and critically evaluate knowledge from a variety of online sources. (para. 5)

This new digital picture of learning creates a very different set of experiences going well beyond curricular content and testing. Learning now is more global, stressing the understanding of international perspectives as well communicating and collaborating with others in different ways. The time to change is now.

Reflecting on the Work
In leading to prepare students for tomorrow . . . 1. Have you discussed the concept of student choice and learner agency when designing your curriculum? 2. Do your students know why they are learning?

WHAT WE KNOW TODAY ABOUT TOMORROW

One of the most significant challenges as we move forward in redesigning schools is to understand how much of what we know today will have an impact on learning for all students tomorrow. In the recent years of No Child Left Behind Act (U.S. Department of Education, 2001), Race to the Top (U.S. Department of Education, 2009), and now the Every Student Succeeds Act (2015), a tremendous focus has been placed on content standards with accountability defined through high-stakes testing.

Few have argued with the need to understand content; however, the critical disconnect is that the skills assessed in current content areas using a selective response schema look very different than those identified as critical for students to be successful in the future. What we know today is that the new learners as described earlier will move through their education system woefully ill-prepared unless we significantly change our thinking.

We are beginning to understand that the complexities of learning are connected to the complexities of who students are as individuals. This shift is a stark contrast from previous generations who saw themselves seeking a better life based on economic stability and job status. Today, students are interested in who they are and how they can contribute to society. While this concept is not discussed in great length, the learning culture for tomorrow will need to be more predicated on the uniqueness of individuals rather than a competition-centric environment.

Specifically, the transformation of education requires a much stronger focus on creativity and individuality that necessitates a rethinking of the competitive systems built at the national, state, and local levels. Students need to be recognized for what they do as individuals and groups rather than being ranked in their class using a competitive testing or grading metric.

To foster new cultures of innovation and creativity, systems that stop comparing students to each other by recognizing their individual uniqueness will develop learning cultures where all students can be successful. In this way, systems are developed for the learner that change the dynamics of schools to a learner-centered experience, rather than today's teacher-centered delivery systems.

The conversations today about the school structure with set class periods, Carnegie units, and a narrowly defined knowledge-based curriculum will only change with substantive redesign. Lanoue (2017) outlines critical topics for discussion as schools move to a learner-centric environment.

- Curricular content should be easily accessible in multiple formats and available anywhere at any time, so that students have access to the content that best meets their interests and personal learning needs.
- Software should be adaptable, helping students to better identify and understand both their academic strengths and growth areas. Proficiency as determined by practice is preferred compared to proficiency determined by test scorers.
- Teachers should use analytics to better identify individual needs and align services and resources to support them.
- Communication tools and social media can connect students to each other and with other students around the world.
- New innovations provide new ways to keep parents informed and engaged.
- Access to information is more equitable and available, which makes it possible for students to collaborate and solve more problems. (para. 13)

Conversations around these topics will help districts design new models to move them from the industrial age and factory model into the network era where communication and access to information redefines the work.

When you look at schools today, very little has changed with the structures that define a student's school day. While we see adjustments in traditional structures such as yearlong schedules to block schedules or longer days and later start times, we see very little else. The new era of learning will be defined by a new focus on students through the lens of emerging technologies and worldwide access. New learning technologies will allow students to communicate more effectively with each other about their learning, and will give them worldwide access to information and people anytime and anywhere. Learning spaces will change, going beyond the walls of the school.

While many believe that the use of technology takes away from the human interaction required in the learning process, learning technologies can create far greater opportunities for collaboration and engagement. Think about when students were in rows, and the teacher started the lesson by saying, "stop talking, you are here to learn." That translates to "you are here to learn from me and not from each other." Or even today at the collegiate level where students are in lecture halls with 300 to 400 students listening—there is not much social interaction within that kind of delivery or level of access.

With learning technologies, schools can expand the social elements of learning and lessen the isolation students often experience. While current tools in social media are mostly seen as a detriment and distraction, schools should think about what would happen if social media were used as a learning construct for communicating, brainstorming, collaborating, and problem solving. Articulating a defined use and attaching a different nomenclature to social media provides for a new understanding of social media, where the uses of social media tools are part of the learning process. This helps students to define this social media space differently.

Students want to share their work across the world and digital tools will allow them to do so. We are in a time where connectivity and information flow is simply large, fast developing, and is now the mainstream in everyone's personal and professional lives. Leaders have a new responsibility to embrace this shift for all students and to initiate new programming where the world is open for students. In so many ways, the world in which we live is shrinking, and worldwide connections for students are increasing, allowing them to be able to create a new understanding of all that surrounds them.

The ability for students to access their education on any day and at any time challenges conventional thinking about existing school structures and the regimen of daily schedules. We know today that students see their work not in periods, weeks, or even years. While self-paced or continuous progress programs are not new, the use of new technology tools, especially those with adaptive learning capabilities, provide the necessary supports, allowing students to take advantage of such programs designed to be self-regulated and information access rich.

Students can navigate their learning and show mastery and understanding without sitting in classrooms or clocking in a set minimum number of hours. Learning cultures developed around new clearly defined skills and standards can create needed consistency while allowing greater flexibility in other structures like the school day, attendance every day, and the challenges associated with the transitions experienced by students that frequently move between schools.

Most district vision and mission statements set a direction for students to be lifelong learners, but school programs often create finite learning opportunities that do not match the world students will enter when they graduate from high school. Preparing students for a new workforce with new skills in problem solving, collaboration, communication, and information access will be paramount in preparing students for the workforce where an estimated 25 percent of the jobs will change during a student's four years in high school. Educational leaders have a unique opportunity to shift school structures and programs to stay ahead of what students will need to be successful.

The Speak Up Research Project for Digital Learning (2017) surveyed over 500,000 thousand people including students, parents, teachers, and school leaders about what skills are most important for students to be successful. Their list of workplace skills looks very different from those we presently define today in our schools. Critical thinking, working with diverse people, teamwork and collaboration, creativity, communication, and the use of technology are at the top of the list. In addition, survey results revealed that schools need to provide students with opportunities to gain work experience through internships or volunteering, participation in leadership and team activities, and effective use of technology within classes while at school.

The conversations about the skills needed for students to be successful has been in many ways muted by the movement of accountability where the primary focus has been on content standards and the use of standardized testing. However, superintendents can no longer wait to have different conversations as change occurs around them. Much information exists today about what is needed to prepare students for their world; yet, superintendents and school leaders are slow to change.

Superintendents have a Herculean task in creating new conversations that will develop and support learning cultures that are not behind, but rather in front, to prepare students for what they need in an ever changing world. When superintendents understand the need for all students to be successful, the primary question that remains to be asked is "what does success look like in our schools?'

Reflecting on the Work

In leading change in a world where student skills have changed . . .

1. Given the skills required for student success in the future, how have your programs changed?
2. How are you planning to change instructional design in your schools over the next five years?

WHY ACCESS IS IMPORTANT

As the needs of the new learner emerge, information access and the ability to communicate and collaborate using digital tools anywhere, anytime, is a priority for education in this country. Many educational experts have predicted that the use of digital tools will create a larger achievement gap; however, this result will only occur if school and community leaders let it happen. Superintendents, therefore, cannot turn a blind eye to the lack of access as an excuse, but rather signal a need to address accessibility of opportunities and resources head on.

The Pew Research Center has been tracking broadband use for the last 15 years as well as the emerging use of mobile devices. In their most recent report (2017), broadband service in homes increased significantly between 2000 and 2010 and at present, it is estimated that three quarters of American homes now have service. Those least likely to have service are families that are economically disadvantaged, elderly, or live in rural areas. The landscape for mobile devices now looks very different.

Today, 95 percent of the adult population has a mobile phone, and 77 percent (and this percentage is increasing) own a smartphone. Reliance on mobile devices for access is most common for young adults and the economically disadvantaged. The takeaway for superintendents in understanding this changing landscape is that access to the web is feasible, with an understanding of the dynamics of both broadband and mobile uses.

Success in a student's world will require them to have access to information so they can explore their interests, access content to create new content, and collaborate with others. The internet is not simply a search engine or a social communication avenue. Establishing internet access requires creativity, at least in the short-term where access in some areas remains difficult. In every way, districts need to work with students and parents to ensure access for all students. This is an area where brokering partnerships with internet and mobile hotspot providers, creating broad-based community access points, and setting up full community funded access can lead to solutions that will create access for all.

Full access to all educational resources is not a new requirement in public education and has been one of the staples of public education in creating equality and equity for all children. Access to the internet is no different. According to Bentley (2017) "closing this digital-use gap for our most at-risk students will require an all-hands-on-deck effort, with schools, government agencies, broadband providers and nonprofits all pitching in to do their part" (para. 8).

The ultimate responsibility for access lies with the school district. In the end, having access using the internet is no different from every student having a textbook—it is the tool students need to access their education. Greater equity for all learners can be realized through equal access.

Reflecting on the Work
In leading change in a world where access can provide equity . . .   1. Have conversations about access led to restrictive or more open environments?   2. What conversations are occurring in your district about technology and access leveling the learning field for students?

THE RISKS IN PLANNING FOR TOMORROW

Leading the transformation of schools may be one of the most daunting tasks for any educational leader due to the traditionalism that centers most schools and districts across the country. No longer can the superintendent "just" manage the operations and be successful. If schools are going to meet the needs of all children, then superintendents will need to navigate a change process knowing the risks from the reactions of both the system's internal and external stakeholders. Effectiveness as a superintendent in the future will be measured by the way navigating change unfolds with internal and external constituents.

Risk Taking Is not Comfortable

For superintendents, taking risks comes with the job, embedded within overall responsibilities. However, taking risks when it comes to reshaping the educational experience for children is not always a comfortable conversation that takes place between superintendents, school boards, parents, and members of the community. Taking risks by challenging traditional structures, even when defined in a district strategic plan creates personal and professional risks for superintendents. To understand more fully, we return to our image of the rubber band.

In many ways, education is like a rubber band. It can change shapes around something but always has a tension to snap back to its original form. Educational leaders are challenged by this phenomenon even if they survived the initial change. We know from the literature that change occurs in stages. Insecurities, resistance, and pushback by internal and external constituents often haunt these stages. Simply stated, change takes us into the unknown.

To be clear, educational leaders must be the models in what they do. Educators continually ask students to take risks, so they can grow and achieve new heights in a way that supports their hopes and dreams. Therefore, if we expect this from our children, then the adults, especially educational leaders, need to determine how they and the system take risk through the design of new programs and processes to ensure that all students are successful.

If districts and schools are going to make fundamental changes so that all students can be successful in their worlds, then risk-taking needs to be part of the equation for planning and practice. For example, many adults believe that not all students can go to college and the system needs to create a dichotomy—one group of students go to college and one group of students go to work after high school graduation.

Risk-taking occurs when systems approach strategic planning from the lens where all students can push themselves with the right supports. In this example, risk-taking is asking a different question. The question is not about going to college or not. The question is, "how do we prepare students to learn and engage beyond high school?" We know that creating programs around different questions is required if districts believe that students need to engage in learning well beyond high school.

Risk-Takers Are Champions

Much rhetoric exists today about schools remaining the same as the school program of the Industrial Age. The leaders who are ready to take the risks for all students are the champions. From the business sector, Rittmanic (2016) recommends three unique qualities in change champions:

- Humility accompanied by a belief that they do not know everything about their business;
- Personal ability to change how they think and operate, including possibly the role they will play in the firm moving forward; and,
- Capacity to be "all in" with supporting transition in their business, which often means operating outside long-held comfort zones. (para. 4)

Champions understand the inherent risks and are able to hold the line when the media outlets, internal and external stakeholders, and political pressure are ratcheted up because traditional or long-held systems are disrupted. Taking action around the true belief that all students can achieve and succeed is "risky" but "required." Superintendents who champion these efforts need to stand united because taking this path alone takes a toll personally and professionally.

In the recent accountability movement, school performance, or lack of it, has been a national focus. High-stakes testing, graduation requirements, subgroup performance, and the disparities between the performances of these subgroups was more than disconcerting—it was alarming. This alarm about the lack of success for all students started many years ago with the report, *Nation at Risk: The Imperative for Educational Reform* (U.S. Department of Education, 1983). The sound of the bell rang more loudly with the legislation that yielded numerous policy reformations when the No Child Left Behind Act (U.S. Department of Education, 2001) defined new accountability measures.

Unfortunately, the rhetoric surrounding the conversations focusing on accountability measures distorts the realities of low-performing students. It is here that the call for change was loud, but for who? The new conversations need to center on the work needed in public schools and its communities to prepare all students for a new world. These types of conversations will more than likely induce apprehension in the community; however, it is worth the risk.

Why Take Risks?

The reform movements that stemmed from federal and state policy continue to fuel conversations, mostly centered on improving test scores that typically result in fringe changes to the structure of schools. Most reforms dealt with modifications in schedules, calendars, instructional time, resource allocation, and instructional practices with a strong focus in the content areas.

One of the significant challenges of superintendents will be how they engage in different conversations other than the current ones. According to the Pew Research Center (2016), the U.S. workplace will see dramatic shifts as the nation moves more into a knowledge-focused age. Students who understand these new needs will likely be rewarded for social, communication, and analytical skills. Most notable in Pew's findings was that current workers report that the pre-K–12 education system was second only to individuals in being responsible for job readiness. This responsibility is one that should drive superintendents in examining closely how and what transformations need to occur to prepare students for what they need.

Creating new conversations and strategic initiatives that support the skills needed in the workforce is not necessarily a new conversation but often the conversations have been more about a segment of the student population seeking careers rather than all students; that is, the dichotomy of some students attending college and other students going to work. Given the pre-K–12 school system's responsibilities for preparing students for what they will need to be successful, even over colleges and universities, is a strong message about the role of pre-K–12 schools. Schools can no longer avoid rethinking instructional design and delivery by making only fringe changes.

Making fringe changes will place students at a significant disadvantage. A different conversation in schools may be jump-started by using key points about the educational requirements to meet the needs of emerging jobs. While there are many risks for superintendents every day in decisions about school operations, budget, policy, and personnel, inevitably some of the riskiest conversations that superintendents will engage in are about changing the school structures to support the needs of all children for a new world.

In the current discussions about transforming education, school districts typically get embroiled in conversations about low standardized test scores, graduation rates, or college acceptance rates. These discussions are important, but not enough, because transforming education is more than test scores and college and career data to frame decisions. In the end, superintendents need to lead the risks with conversations about the skills defined for future work while recognizing these attributes will constantly be changing to keep pace moving forward.

Reflecting on the Work

In leading change in a world that is risky for school leaders . . .

1. How have you led conversations about transforming schools to support new skills?
2. How do you see all students as having equal opportunity to succeed after high school?

SUMMARY

Parents and community members seldom see the direct work of schools in laying the foundations for the careers of their children. They often see pre-K–12 education and postsecondary education as an endpoint into the job market. However, if schools are to prepare students with different skills for changing careers, then schools as seen today will need to be redefined with radically different systems designed and implemented.

Creating different conversations about the success of all students in their world and redefining systems must take on a very different shape—one that will be the utmost challenge to lead. In the end, access to learning changes everything about what we do today. That is why transformational superintendents will need to be resolute in redefining their roles in reconstructing schools, and they need to be fearless about what is needed for all students to succeed in their world—not ours.

In redesigning schools, the voice of the superintendents must be strong but cannot be the voice of one. Chapter 6 describes how the voice of the superintendent works in tandem with the community to support the work of schools and how the power of social media outlets can be an asset in school transformation.

A SUPERINTENDENT'S DIVE INTO LEADING IN A WORLD OF ACCESS

1. Create opportunities with your school board to talk about the workplace of the future and the skills required for students to be successful. Evaluate how these conversations affect your strategic plan.
2. Develop a learning profile for students in your district and define the skills they would need to be successful. Evaluate school programs to determine if they support these skills for all students.
3. Evaluate how students in your district have internet access and establish a timeline to ensure access for all students.

SUGGESTED READINGS

Bryk, A. S., Gomez, L. M., Grunow, A., & LeMahieu, P.G. (2015). *Learning to improve: How America's schools can get better at getting better*. Cambridge, MA: Harvard Education Press.

Garvey Berger, J., & Johnston, K. (2015). *Simple habits for complex times: Powerful practices for leaders*. Stanford, CA: Stanford University Press.

Supovitz, J. A., & Spillane, J. P. (2015). *Challenging standards: Navigating conflict and building capacity in the era of the Common Core*. Lanham, MD: Rowman & Littlefield.

Wilhoit, G., Pittenger, L., & Rickabaugh, J. (2016). *Leadership for Learning: What is leadership's role in supporting success for every student?* Lexington, KY: Center for Innovation in Education.

REFERENCES

Bentley, K. (2017, June 14). Home internet access for all students is a game-changer [Blog]. Center for Digital Education. Retrieved from http://www.centerdigitaled.com/blog/home-internet-access.html

Education Reimagined. (2015). *A transformational vision for education in the U.S.* Washington, DC: Convergence Center for Policy Resolution. Retrieved from http://education-reimagined.org/wp-content/uploads/2015/10/A-Transformational-Vision-for-Education-in-the-US-2015-09.pdf

Every Student Succeeds Act. (2015). Pub. L. 114-95, 129 Stat. 1802.

Lanoue, P. D. (2017, September 5). To create a learner-centric culture, understand the story behind every face. [Blog]. *Course Correction. TrustED.* Retrieved from http://trustedk12.com/course-correction-learner-centric-school-leadership/

Mahaffie, J. B. (2017). *Nine skills that will help make our children future-ready.* [Blog]. *WISE ed.review.* Retrieved from http://www.wise-qatar.org/john-mahaffie-learning-future-job-skills

Nellie Mae Education Foundation. (n.d.). *Student centered approaches.* Retrieved from https://www.nmefoundation.org/our-vision

New Learning. (n.d.). The new school. *New Learning—Transformational Designs for Pedagogy and Assessment.* Retrieved from http://newlearningonline.com/learning-by-design/the-new-school

No Child Left Behind Act. 2001. Pub. L. 107-110, 115 Stat. 1425, as amended by 20 U.S.C. § 6301.

Pew Research Center. (2016, October 6). *The state of American jobs: How the shifting economic landscape is reshaping work and society and affecting the way people think about the skills and training they need to get ahead.* Washington, DC: Pew Research Center. Retrieved from http://www.pewsocialtrends.org/2016/10/06/the-state-of-american-jobs/

Pew Research Center. (2017). *Internet/broadband fact sheet.* Washington, DC: Pew Research Center. Retrieved from http://www.pewinternet.org/fact-sheet/internet-broadband/

Rittmanic, M. (2016). *Three characteristics needed to champion change.* Lead Change Group—A Division of Weaving Influence. Retrieved from http://leadchangegroup.com/three-characteristics-needed-to-champion-change/

The Speak Up Research Project for Digital Learning. (2017). *From Blackboard Innovation Series.* Retrieved from http://www.tomorrow.org/speakup/Connecting-Dots-for-Digital-Learning_pres.html

U.S. Department of Education. (1983). *A nation at risk: The imperative for education reform.* A report to the nation and the Secretary of Education. Washington, DC: U.S. Department of Education.

U.S. Department of Education. (2009). *Race to the Top program: Executive summary.* Washington, DC: U.S. Department of Education. Retrieved from https://www2.ed.gov/programs/racetothetop/index.html

Chapter 6

The Voice of the Superintendent

IN THIS CHAPTER . . .

- Relationships and Connecting with Communities
- Your Beliefs and Those of Your Community
- Activism and Who Hears You
- Social Media
- A Market-Driven Culture
- The Media Risks

LETTER FROM THE SUPERINTENDENT

Dear School and District Leaders:

Our discussion last week on how we can best use social media tools as a communication vehicle for our schools and district brought forward many divergent opinions. We have leaders at different ends of the spectrum and strong voices from supporters and critics of social media. However, we walked away with complete agreement that we need to know and own our messages.

I have always positioned myself to ensure that as a district we remain current in our practices, model the practices that were best for our students and community, and take risks to become better at our work. One of the district goals for the year is to improve communication and work to ensure the greatest transparency to parents and the community in what we do. In this day where information flow is fast, it is my position that we must forge ahead with developing policies and designing systems where social media outlets will be foundational to our communication plan.

As I reflected on the concerns and came to this decision about the uses of social media, I kept going back to an article by Hardy (2014). In this article, Hardy quotes Ann Flynn, director of education technology for the National School Board Association, who said "simply . . . sitting on the sidelines is not an option. If you don't get online, someone else will become the 'official' district website. Ignoring it will allow someone else to take over your 'brand'—and your district is your brand" (2014, p. 11).

We are the brand of our district and cannot be on the sidelines. We must not only keep pace with technology for communication, but we must also become leaders in the field. As we develop our skills, please keep in mind that as educators, we model the skills we want our students and parents to use.

As always, thank you for freely sharing your thoughts.

Sincerely,

Superintendent

The new role of the superintendent is much larger than running the operations of their school districts and must extend well beyond the school walls if schools and their communities are going to be successful. For many years, public education systems remained relatively insular and kept much to themselves in educating children. Students moving into jobs that did not require a high school diploma were readily available in the industry sector and only required a student's readiness to learn on the job. The thinking was, "if students wanted an education, then schools would give that to them, but if they did not want an education then they should go to work." This dichotomy in thinking—education or work—where dropouts could get a job, is over!

The impact of recent reform movements that relied on high-stakes testing results and school ratings has placed schools in a very different spotlight resulting in state and federal legislators wanting increased control of schools through legislative actions. The legislative culture both on the federal and state levels has positioned superintendents and school leaders in a new role. Superintendents must now engage at every level of their communities and with legislators at the state and federal levels to provide accurate information that influences policy, and law.

School success along with the political appetite to change education is now directly influenced by social media which is here to stay. The information flow through social media outlets can no longer be isolated or blocked in its use by students or adults. According to the Pew Research Center (2017), social media usage has increased significantly with over 69 percent of the public in the United States engaging in social media outlets. Leaders may think that the challenges of social media are mostly about students or localized to certain demographics. Social media involves everyone in the system.

Without politically engaged superintendents who understand the power of social media and who have strong voices for all children, laws and policies will become more exclusionary than inclusionary under the cloaking of "for all children." With a shift of control returning more to the state level, it is incumbent on superintendents to impact decisions at every level.

RELATIONSHIPS AND CONNECTING WITH COMMUNITIES

Schools cannot do this work alone. Shifting communities, as described in chapter 3, experience changing dynamics influenced by poverty, mobility, and shifting demographics, resulting in communities being more diverse culturally and ethnically. While much work in recent years has focused on the internal workings of schools and school districts to improve the performance of all students, improving student achievement cannot be realized by schools in isolation.

Superintendents will need to exercise greater leadership in the community to make connections and to form working relationship with business, civic, and faith-based organizations that share common interest in supporting the education of children. The new work is much more than attending community meetings or serving on boards. Rather, the work centers on developing very deliberate and defined plans on how outside organizations can support schools. However, to attend to this work, superintendents will need to create new internal structures because schools are not well-designed to create outside collaborative models.

Accessing resources from community agencies and organizations may be the most significant untapped asset that can be used to support the work of schools. Historically, schools have sporadic approaches to accessing community resources in their planning, often because schools have not always been structured to take advantage of what communities have to offer. Today, schools can no longer do it alone. Successful systems will need to develop ways to open the doors—requiring a new leadership role for the superintendent.

Businesses and Industry

History reflects an increasing bond with business and industry through the establishment of the Carl D. Perkins Vocational and Applied Technology Education Act Amendments of 1990 that outlined vocational education opportunities at the secondary level. In addition, the business and manufacturing communities had considerable influence on programs and decisions through their involvement on advisory boards or job internships. Vocational/ technical education in many ways continued to promote a dichotomy—those that went to college or those that went directly into the workforce or were prepared with "life skills." The primary focus for business and manufacturing industries was to prepare a workforce for their own companies.

Today, business and industry have begun to see their role more as supporting young adults differently than simply wanting to train them to be part of their workforce. They see themselves as mentors and adult role models who have a new responsibility in preparing students with the skills and confidence to be successful. With a new direction, business and industry have joined together to support students in being good citizens who have the confidence and soft skills to navigate the many decisions through high school and their postsecondary choices—regardless of whether they work for their company.

Local Government

One of the relationships that is changing quickly is between schools and local governments. Two factors have influenced the need to have greater collaboration at the local level. The first is the positioning of communities to be economically competitive to attract the business sectors. The second is school performance ratings used by parents to make decisions on where to live. These two conditions have placed both organizations in a position where neither can afford not to work with each other.

Local governments, like school governance entities, have primary responsibility for developing and monitoring operations and for engaging in short- and long-term planning. Both schools and local governmental agencies have very similar roles that exist within common boundaries. School districts and local governments as well as other agencies must be able to work in tandem. It is through this work that vibrancy filters throughout the community.

Superintendents must recognize the power of working to facilitate strong relationships because education is a significant part of the fabric required for healthy communities. When schools work in isolation, they are not meeting the needs of their communities. When neighborhoods fail to grow and develop, the result is in greater poverty and community disarray. On the positive side, when schools work with local governmental agencies, education can be a key catalyst for community revitalization.

Politics and Political Mapping

Many educators including leaders often shy away from politics with the typical statement, "I am not a politician. I just run my school district or teach in my classroom." Simply put, "These days are over!" In the last several decades, education has been significantly influenced through legislation and political coalitions that have carved themselves into what many perceive as the "education industry."

Today, the ability for districts to make individual decisions is becoming more limited given the provisions outlined through federal and state legislation. Ideas and movements to reform schools are modeled after business systems and antiquated metrics for effectiveness. The information flow to decision-makers is often ignored for other less genuine interests to change direction for the good of all children. Superintendents need to be center in this political arena.

Legislators need more information to understand legislative impact, and superintendents can and must be that source of information. Since the changes in education will continue to be central in the political arena, superintendents must position themselves to be significant voices for their schools and education at the local, state, and national levels. Regular meetings with local governance groups including mayors, commissioners, and city or county managers establish strong working bonds when based on a level of openness and trust. In both the short- and long-term, clarity and unity in direction enable schools to make needed changes, often minimizing pushback and resistance.

When navigating the political arena (political mapping), taking hard positions against individuals can become problematic very quickly. Personal attacks will likely, in the end, come back to negatively affect you and the district. Constructive dialogue that includes alternate solutions to the problems targeted by policy and law have the greatest ability to bring perspective and understanding to the process of finding solutions.

Superintendents have a critical role in working with their boards and community, so they understand the issues and the potential impact on their schools. Establishing positions on issues that are agreed on by the board sends strong messages to the community about the joint voice of the superintendent and board on key issues. The voice of the superintendent becomes amplified when joined by the voices of the board and the community.

Discussing perspectives and alternate solutions in the public is more powerful and lends greater credibility. In a white paper presented to the Georgia Department of Education on concerns about the state evaluation system for teachers, the Teacher Keys Evaluation System (TKES) and the Leader Keys Evaluation System (LKES) for principals, concerns were addressed (Lanoue & Zepeda, 2014). However, before addressing these concerns, the work on these processes were recognized as a way of setting the stage for different options related to teacher and leader evaluation.

We are pleased for the opportunity to provide insights for change based on the strengths gained from what we know about practice, policy, and research. First, we establish that there are elements of TKES and LKES that reflect sound research and practitioner practices. TKES is certainly a much-needed update from the Georgia Teacher Evaluation Program (GTEP). However, it is also our opinion that there are critical implementation flaws in the TKES and LKES processes that could be addressed within the regulations defined by H.B. 244. (Lanoue & Zepeda, 2014, p. 2)

Lanoue and Zepeda then continue to outline the issues:

Primarily, our major concerns relate to TKES, which relies heavily on single and poorly-constructed measures of performance indicators for student growth and then applies the single measure to determine 50 percent of a teacher's performance. By fiat, TKES has become a value-added system with its over-reliance on high-stakes testing. (p. 2)

By providing perspective that recognizes the work at the legislative level is critical if the superintendent's recommendations will be seen as credible and not simply complaining.

However, there are times when superintendents know when they need to take a stance regardless of the fallout. The superintendent's voice needs to ring loud when the need arises to protect students, teachers, and the community. In these situations, clarity with conviction sends the message needed. As an example, the opening line of a blog by Lanoue (2015) published in the *Washington Post* on excessive testing opened with a clear statement, "We are in the midst of a testing epidemic. We are requiring teachers to give students test after test, and students are asking who the test evaluates—because it is not about them anymore" (para. 3).

The voices of superintendents must be strong and loud with perspective and advocacy for their districts; however, this voice must be balanced. Opposition on issues can bring perspectives that can be perceived as an attack on individuals or their work. Every superintendent should understand the need to traverse this ground carefully especially in public settings. No legislator or state official wants to read about a superintendent bashing him/her on issues.

Community Organizations

Resources for communities can be found in its nonprofit and faith-based organizations. Often, these organizations are not part of a district support network and mostly function independently of schools in their support of children and their families. In addition, communities will typically see an overlap in resources as nonprofit organizations may have similar missions with most having some role in supporting children and their success in education.

Superintendents can demonstrate the importance of community resources by including outside agencies in the fabric of the districts strategic plan. In this way, school districts maximize community support services by strategically coordinating efforts. While this might take some resources on the side of the district, the return is tremendous when schools know how readily to access community support for their children and families.

Developing a culture of mutualism where community organizations come together to provide wraparound services for families requires the superintendent to take the lead by developing processes to help groups to create common goals and to develop supports that overlap resources. When community organizations suggest promising ideas, or they develop unique collaborative opportunities to help schools, superintendents need to find ways for their systems to take advantage of these opportunities.

Faith-Based Organizations

One of the largest untapped resource in communities is faith-based organizations. Public schools have traditionally narrowed the working relationship with these organizations in efforts to maintain the separation of church and state guidelines. Given the tenor of the times and the wide range of social media, a religious frenzy in schools can create a substantive distraction if not approached in a way that is all about a partnership to support students and their families.

Creating the dialogue with faith-based leaders about their role in the community can lead to unique programs that help make connections for families with young children. Superintendents will need to take risks and navigate the fears of religion in schools by finding the "right" space where both organizations can seamlessly work collaboratively to support their children and families. Shared space to support teachers and children can be created through common interest and involvement that is not in conflict with the rulings on the separation of church and state.

Colleges and Universities

The conversations around the preparation of teachers and school leaders continues to be a focus across our country and many superintendents have concerns about their distant relationship with surrounding colleges and universities related to the level of preparedness of teacher and leader candidates. There exist many disconnects in the working relationships between postsecondary institutions and the pre-K–12 education sector—often delineated by a lack of understanding between researchers and practitioners. It is here where the connections between research and practice can support change for both organizations.

Let's get to the point. If the institutions that educate children and the institutions that prepare teachers and leaders to work with children cannot work together, then education in this country has a significant issue. If not resolved, both institutions will fail to meet their mission—to conduct research on new practices and prepare and support teachers, leaders, and other professionals to meet the learning needs of children. The back-and-forth bantering about the ability to connect research and practice is still a chronic issue. The result is that education often lacks a widely used research base to create new practices or to sustain existing ones. The responsibility for this disconnect lies equally with both institutions and more directly with their leaders.

How do these institutions move forward, together? The first and most vital step is where the adults in these organizations understand and embrace the value of research and practice and that the exchange of information and ideas goes equally both ways. The stance that one institution can "fix" the other simply will not work. Only when both institutions share in what they know and can do, will the work influence what occurs in classrooms.

Reflecting on the Work

In leading your community with a strong voice . . .

1. Reflect on your relationship with the business community. Is the focus on preparing workers or is there a broader focus for the development of youth?
2. In what ways do you and/or your board have a voice in local, state, and national politics?

YOUR BELIEFS AND THOSE OF YOUR COMMUNITY

School districts plan and make decisions around organizational beliefs typically agreed upon by the school board or governing body. Creating a set of beliefs should include input from those that work in the district and from the community that the schools serve. Organizational beliefs are critical to the school district's health, vitality, and ability to plan. Most policy and program issues come under fire or are challenged based on conflicts in organizational decisions that do not support or are perceived not to support its beliefs. It is here that superintendents stay awake at night, trying to balance their own beliefs with the system and community beliefs when making tough decisions.

Superintendents should continuously ensure district and school practices align to district beliefs, especially in working with system and school leaders. In addition, superintendents should create opportunities for parents and community leaders to engage in conversations about beliefs and actions. The right conversations are created when leaders reflect on their beliefs, the district's beliefs, and their actions. The end goal is to bring coherence between what is believed to occur and what occurs in supporting district beliefs.

Reflecting on the Work
In leading your community with a strong voice . . . 1. What actions do you take when leader decisions at the district and school levels are made that do not align to the system's beliefs? 2. Reflect on a program decision that was derailed. Was it aligned to your beliefs, and was that part of the discussion?

ACTIVISM AND WHO HEARS YOU

Superintendents as well as district and school leaders will need to carve out roles in this new space of being active and leading an activist's role. The politics around education continue to be fierce and often less aligned to benefit all children. The tensions have become so great that the largest polarizing impact may be inherent in political policy rather than ideology. Educational leaders will have no choice but to navigate the tensions of politics and ideologies with a voice of reason and direction. It is in this space where influence and credibility prevail, so change can be made and sustained.

In this environment of bashing public schools, district leaders have been silenced in many ways. Their voices have been muted under the guise of not wanting to change or the desire to maintain the status quo, thus perpetuating failing systems. Often the tensions are created when leaders defend programs that may not serve a need for some students but are unable to have answers for the other students not being served well.

One of the first moves a superintendent should make is to understand the politics at the local level first and soon thereafter at the state level. This understanding of the political landscape can only come from engaging in many conversations, reading historical documents, and listening to a variety of constituents. However, even with the best political mapping, superintendents will need to gain valuable credibility that is garnered in that shared space between being active and then engaging in activism.

Superintendents have an immediate opportunity to create pockets of activism as the secretary to the school board. School boards can have a profound influence if they assume the right role and act as one. Individual board members who become politically active for their own agenda, yet represent the board, are certainly problematic and in every way, this kind of role diminishes the credibility a board has established in times with politically charged agendas. When the board speaks as one on an issue, their active voice can influence decisions at all levels.

The critical juncture for board activism lies in what the board wants to support related to governance and changes in rules or legislation. Positioning on pending legislation can create polarizing effects in the community that may not help the board in their ability to make good decisions about their district or to develop broad community support. Therefore, it is good practice not to take stances on individual legislative pieces but rather to take stances on the principles or perceived impacts of any changes that legislators should consider.

Even in the most politically charged environments, superintendents and school boards need to take positions at every level and these positions should also support priorities for other organizations. For superintendents, guiding the board is extremely important. Superintendents must tread strategically to ensure that the tensions created do not fracture or discredit the board.

Superintendents, your voice must be the loudest and strongest if we expect to educate all children in this country. The challenge in creating your voice remains with the level of credibility garnered in the everyday conversations and the trust established at the local level and beyond. Superintendents often stay awake at night reflecting on their beliefs about the work that needs to be done and about how to navigate bringing communities together with one voice. Moreover, the alignment of beliefs with actions weigh heavily when superintendents are vocal and "present" in the work needed in their communities and at the state and national stage.

Reflecting on the Work
In leading your community with a strong voice . . . 1. Have you taken positions on educational issues, and how have these positions been communicated? 2. How does your school board influence state and federal policy?

SOCIAL MEDIA

The implications of social media will be challenging to superintendents because many are entering an unknown space. In addition, supporters and critics are already lining up to influence social media's role in the school environment. The decisions made by leaders will be pivotal in how social media influences learning and the overall culture of the system. Given the complexities and varying positions, superintendents will just have to find ways to use social media to transform their systems. To carry this out, persistent conversations about social media trends, processes, and policies will need to be part of a superintendent's everyday discussion.

Due to the public nature of schools and its operations, superintendents strive for their district's communications to be as transparent as possible with the primary goal to keep the public informed of school operations and activities. However, with the increased use of public media outlets, several shifts are occurring that put superintendents in a challenging position.

The first shift is the desire for the current population to get information instantly. With students and adults having 24-hour, anytime access to information, time becomes a critical factor in the release of information. If districts cannot find ways to communicate quickly to its public, then the public will control the message. By not giving the quick release of information, districts will come under intense pressure for their inability to communicate in a timely fashion.

The second issue becomes deciding what information is pertinent, valid, and open to all. The concept of transparency becomes challenging because districts most often limit information to protect students and personnel. Districts that make protective statements about information that cannot be released, often come under fire for "hiding" information. System leaders are accused of being less transparent, when in reality; they are often giving more information than in the past before the emergence of social media.

Superintendents are challenged by the information flow from outside the system that is inaccurate and perhaps filled with biases. Countering these types of situations typically leads to perceived excuses and often sets up a scenario of who says what and what do you believe? In developing a plan for institutional transparency, Smiciklas (2013) recommends that systems use multiple social media outlets to establish the greatest "ease" of access. Social media plans enhance organizational transparency by using new communication streams, giving factual and correct information, recognizing diverse views, and creating a hub for information.

Even with a clear plan and professional learning for leaders, the transition to social media transparency will bring trepidation for its leaders. Leaders often question what is shared and how their communications are interpreted when using social media outlets. At the forefront of thought and action, educational leaders must be protective of their students and the messages about their schools. With effective social media plans, leaders can establish trust by quickly providing helpful and timely information through their communication outlets.

A Leader's Presence

When leaders make a commitment to use social media, what are the implications for changes in leadership characteristics? With an increasing demand on transparency and the flow of information, superintendents are placed in a position that requires rethinking because no longer can information come from the top and trickle down into the system. In many ways, superintendents need to think about messaging of both the system and their roles in leading them. No longer are roles and messages vertical or linear—they are circular and must be malleable.

Shifting Leader Qualities

In the era of social media, Notter (n.d.) describes a leadership change from one of a focus on the institution to a focus on individuals. Leadership characteristics shift from holding people accountable and leveraging best practices to one of a more human perspective where leaders embrace change and are open to innovative ideas. In a social-media–rich environment, "the more proactive leaders can be in shifting . . . leadership and management practices to become more open, trustworthy, generative, and courageous, the more effective they will be in the shift to social media" (Notter, n.d., para. 8).

In the current view, controlling or influencing social media remains a priority to ensure accurate information is made available to communities with superintendents feeling compelled to respond to all the messages that are pushed out about the system, its programs, or personnel. That level of involvement will make superintendents weary. Patience of response must prevail in identifying the elusive point of interception. Most are aware that in this age, to fan the fires is to respond constantly to inaccuracies or different points-of-view, and the flames will only get bigger and brighter. Having a strong social media plan along with patience may be the best advice for superintendents.

Table 6.1. Leadership Actions in Building Cultures of Change Using Social Media

Leadership Actions	Impact
Communicate	Leaders can readily communicate change and get feedback. Members of the system have a voice and feel engaged.
Collaborate	Unleashes creativity and creates conversations on key topics that are important to leaders and the organization.
Educate	Gives members of the organization access to the best thinking around the world. Provides needed information quickly and allows questioning for clarification.
Engage	Allows leaders to engage on a more personal level that helps build morale resulting in happier employees.
Monitor	Leaders can get a pulse of what is happening in the organizations and adjustments are made with information from broader sources.
Maximize	Information is gathered from the wide range of sources with a growing use of social media tools.
Enjoy	Social media allows employees to express themselves and creates excitement and joy when coming to work.

Adapted from Biro (2013, paras. 3–10)

Tools for Supporting Change

While social media in the education world has mostly been relegated to communication flow around information about the district and to handle issues or crises that arise, social media can also be a powerful tool for helping leaders transform their districts and schools. Social media can help districts build community and voice where the information flow is two-way, promoting interaction between leaders and the communities served.

Biro (2013) sees the use of social media for leaders as a way to stimulate and build a cohesive and active culture in their organizations. Table 6.1 identifies and briefly describes social media actions for leaders.

When school districts go through changes, making the connection to all in the system is critical. Everyone wants to be knowledgeable, and through social media, superintendents can close the information gap between employees within the system as well as the gaps across communities.

Engaging in the use of social media creates a new presence for superintendents and school leaders. Entering this space is not one that is comfortable nor easy with its vastness in connecting to the world, emergence of new social media tools, and the personal and professional risks involved by being more transparent and open. However, using social media to transform leadership is no longer an option—in many ways, social media is a requirement for survival.

Reflecting on the Work

In your social media strategies . . .

1. How do you analyze and evaluate social media use from inside and outside of the system?
2. Identify your concerns about the use of social media and develop strategies to get more information related to resolving these concerns.

A MARKET-DRIVEN CULTURE

Looking back historically, districts and their schools were typically known by their logo, mascot, or a unique byline that typically related to athletics or some other extracurricular activity that was unique. Today, branding is so much more, causing school leaders to change their mindset as well as the processes in marketing their districts.

In this arena, districts can learn much about branding from the business sector because they have been at the forefront of survival in a market-driven culture. Malaure (2017) underscores the importance of branding:

> Your school's brand is its calling card to the outside world: it's how you're iden-
> tified and remembered. When somebody sees your logo or your school colors,
> it immediately evokes an emotion in them, whether that's admiration, indiffer-
> ence or something else depends on your reputation and how you have marketed
> yourself. (para. 1)

Regardless of context, evoking "emotions" becomes one of the most powerful results of good branding. The processes of branding can propel the district in new directions within the community, providing members with a sense of trust and importance. However, there are pros and cons related to branding.

Should You Rebrand—or Not?

Creating a school brand is a complex and inclusive process, and superintendents should proceed with a level of caution in branding, especially when they want to change the perceptions of the school district. It is critical to understand that changing the "cover" of the district book may influence the internal workings of the school, but branding alone will not cause deep systemic change in the system. Branding to change the image of the school district is ineffective unless internal changes are enacted to improve the system.

When do school districts and schools rebrand themselves? For superintendents, this question is the most critical one, and requires much

Table 6.2. Considerations for Branding or Not

Reasons to Rebrand	Reasons Not to Rebrand
Your communications—print and digital—don't look and sound like you.	You have a new CEO or CMO and he or she wants to make sure the world knows it.
You've evolved, but your brand hasn't.	You have a product or service that's not sufficiently compelling.
Your customers' expectations of how a brand in your space should look, mean, and behave have changed.	You have operational issues in your marketing, sales, or communication areas.
You're transforming your organization.	You want to present yourself as an organization that you can't credibly be, or become.
You've grown through mergers and acquisitions, but does anyone understand who you are now?	You're looking for a successful "Hail Mary!" pass: other things you've tried have not worked.

Adapted from Sametz (n.d., a, paras. 6–11) and Sametz (n.d., b, paras. 7–12)

thought as to the motivation, rationale, and expected outcome of such an effort. Schools and districts often have legacies and history that need to be preserved and protected; yet, in an emerging field of competition, district leaders need to determine if there is a need for rallying change. Sametz (n.d.a, n.d.b) outlines considerations for business leaders on why organizations should consider changing their brand, and why organizations should not consider rebranding as illustrated in table 6.2.

Importance of the Process

Creating a successful brand should be used to communicate and to motivate those inside the system. Branding efforts must recognize the value of those who dedicate themselves every day to the work of educating all students. Therefore, superintendents should do their research and develop a process that captures what needs to be accomplished.

While many might view branding as something to help districts gain support from outside of the system, superintendents should understand that the process of branding starts from within the district. Branding is an inside-out process and not an outside-in process.

Mission and Vision Statements

Starting with a district's vision, mission, and beliefs or values, a district's brand serves to define the direction of the system. Parrotte (2017) recommends that districts vision, mission, and values become the soul of the organization's brand—it humanizes the work of the district.

However, C. Johnson (2016) asserts that organizations need to go beyond their vision (the what) and the mission (the how) by aligning branding to the purpose of the organization's existence. If organizations have a clear vision and mission, branding efforts can have more "horsepower" in driving the work of the district. Di Somma (2013) shares that vision and mission statements are now obsolete, and the brand purpose really should drive an organization because:

> It gives each person a reason to be proud. It calibrates and guides thinking. It's impatient. It's optimistic. It's the benchmark against which all actions are measured.
> The old benchmark: What purpose does this task/idea/approach serve?
> The new benchmark: How does this task/idea/approach serve our purpose? (para. 4)

Creating a clear purpose through branding is a contemporary way for superintendents to communicate key messages about their districts.

Most school districts remain committed to a strong vision and mission for their organization because that is what brings clarity for the community in where they are going and how they will get there. Branding alignment is critical as it sends the right messages—branding is inextricably connected to a district's vision and mission. Some organizations have taken a different approach where the introduction of branding may be the primary driver in transforming the district. In this approach, school district actions and decisions would be driven more by their brand and not the vision and its mission statements.

Reflecting on the Work

In branding your school district . . .

1. Explain how your brand reflects the messages and emotions of the work in your district.
2. Identify the steps that can be taken to make developing a brand more inclusive.

THE MEDIA RISKS

System Risks

Designing a learning landscape using social media creates a vulnerability for both students and employees requiring new monitoring and protection systems to be in place. While the public often has initial concerns about the cost of technology, the larger issue is that social media erases the school boundaries that traditionally have been categorized as "inside of school responsibilities" and "outside of school responsibilities." In the old world, schools could more easily say it did not happen in schools, so it is not our problem. Now with social media, it is the school's problem.

Opening the door to new liabilities because of open access requires new policies to ensure the safety of all in the system. While effective social media use policies help districts to navigate the ever changing liabilities for school districts, striking the balance is not easy. Policies alone without a clear direction can be restrictive and limit the expected value in using social media. Moore (2017) suggests that one of the first steps for systems in using social media is to understand that there are risks. Moore's best advice is, "don't wing it" (para. 12).

Leader Liability

The most obvious risks for every leader is that the overall responsibility of their district now includes creating a system of transparency, where leaders assume much more liability for the actions of others. Often information creates a need for more information to minimize incorrect interpretation analogous to the "telephone game" where messaging becomes distorted as it moves through the communication stream. Leaders will be placed in a difficult position when describing the actions of others, clarifying misinformation, or viewed as stripping the protections of their students (e.g., free speech).

Leaders may be the most vulnerable if they do not become social media savvy as their districts move past them. No school leader should be left behind! When leaders become social media leaders, they can better position themselves to manage its risks as well as strengthening their school district's position in the community. N. Johnson (2016) offers six steps that leaders should consider as they transform themselves into social media leaders. These steps have been adapted to fit the district context and the work of superintendents. The six steps are:

1. *Take personal ownership of social media strategy.* Take personal ownership to drive social media success across their school district—starting with understanding the significance of social media communication strategy. It is more than setting up a media account; it is being engaged and accountable for what is being said.
2. *Listen to what your students, parents, employees, and community are sharing online.* Step back, and take stock of insights by those in the systems and in the community. Leaders can use these insights to connect

with community members, parents, students, and employees at the right time and with the right message.

3. *Be active on at least one social media platform.* Be actively engaged on social networks to reap the true benefits of social media. It is important to start with one account and select the platform that's right for you.

4. *Share compelling stories.* Be positioned to share the district's story and connect with a large audience. It is important to share stories that are both personal and professional in nature, and to limit what you say about the district statistics and its performance metrics.

5. *Emulate the success of others.* Follow what others say on social media outlets who are posting content on a regular basis, and see what types of content they are sharing, what time they are sharing it, and how much people are engaging with it (for example, through "shares" and "likes").

6. *Be authentic.* Remain authentic and transparent, and avoid outsourcing social media tasks to marketing team members. Communications are like talking to a friend and not overshadowed by jargon. (para. 14)

When superintendents open the door to social media, there certainly exists a darker side that must be understood. It is inevitable that the risks and perils of social media will not diminish but can be overshadowed when leaders are thoughtful, open, clear, and accept their roles.

Reflecting on the Work
In understanding the risks . . .   1. What conversations have occurred to identify the system risks with social media and the system's reactions to these risks?   2. How do you balance the social media impact as a leader through the communication of personal and professional information?

SUMMARY

Social media can help to create and support a positive culture through change, provide direction through branding, and establish and drive communication with internal and external stakeholders. For superintendents to navigate the system requires a strong voice through planned political mapping that takes time, patience, and compromise as well as a strong voice captured through social media.

Chapter 7 outlines the role of the superintendent in designing governance models and protocols with their school boards to keep the focus on performance while minimizing the distractions that often come with change.

A SUPERINTENDENT'S DIVE INTO THEIR VOICE

1. List the partnerships established in your community to support youth development. Identify and create new partnerships to provide additional supports and resources.
2. Identify one or two legislative actions that could support the work in your district. Create conversations in your community to gather perspective and compose a position paper identifying the issue and recommendations that can be communicated to your community and legislators.
3. Describe your brand and identify the attributes of the district that the brand communicates. Next, identify the social media strategies that are effective and those that are not effective in this work. Make changes.

SUGGESTED READINGS

Blank, M. J., Jacobson, R., & Melaville, A. (2012). *Achieving results through community school partnerships: How district and community leaders are building effective, sustainable relationships.* Washington, DC: The Center for American Progress.

Council for Corporate & School Partnerships. (2014). *A how-to guide for school-business partnerships.* Atlanta, GA: Council for Corporate & School Partnerships. Retrieved from http://www.nhscholars.org/School-Business%20How_to_Guide. pdf

Mapp, K. L., & Kuttner, P. J. (2013). *Partners in education: A dual capacity-building framework for family-school partnerships.* Austin, TX: Southwest Educational Development Laboratory.

Magette, K. (2014). *Embracing social media: A practical guide to manage risk and leverage opportunity.* Lanham, MD: Rowman & Littlefield.

REFERENCES

Biro, M. M. (2013, November 17). 7 characteristics of a school leader. [Blog]. *Forbes*. Retrieved from https://www.forbes.com/sites/meghanbiro/2013/11/17/7-characteristics-of-a-social-leader/#6208c7eb12a7

Carl D. Perkins Vocational and Applied Technology Education Act Amendments. (1990). Pub. L. 101-392. Retrieved from https://www.govtrack.us/congress/bills/101/hr7

Di Somma, M. (2013, September 11). *Brand building: Purpose vs. vision and mission*. [Blog]. Atlanta, GA: The Blake Project. Branding Strategy Insider. Retrieved from https://www.brandingstrategyinsider.com/2013/09/brand-building-purpose-vs-vision-and-mission.html#.WdKuUUyZO3c

Hardy, L. (2014). School leaders and social media. *American School Board Journal*. 10–13. Retrieved from http://www.asbj.com/MainMenuCategory/Archive/2014/February/0214pdfs/Social-Media-from-the-Top.aspx

Johnson, C. (2016, September 16). *The difference between brand purpose, vision and mission*. [Blog]. Parker, CO: Type A Communications. Retrieved from http://typeacommunications.com/difference-between-brand-purpose-vision-mission/

Johnson, N. (2016, July 20). *6 ways for CEOs to become more actively engaged in social media*. [Blog]. Medford, NJ: EContent Magazine. Retrieved from http://www.econtentmag.com/Articles/Editorial/Commentary/6-Ways-for-CEOs-to-Become-More-Actively-Engaged-on-Social-Media-112157.htm

Lanoue, P. D. (2015, August 27). High stakes testing—the fool's gold of accountability. [Blog]. *Washington Post*. Retrieved at https://www.washingtonpost.com/news/answer-sheet/wp/2015/08/27/2015-superintendent-of-the-year-high-stakes-testing-is-the-fools-gold-of-accountability/?utm_term=.77434581cadf

Lanoue, P. D., & Zepeda, S. J. (2014). *Recommendations on improving teaching and learning by improving teacher and leader effectiveness*. A white paper presented to the Georgia House of Representatives and the Georgia Department of Education. Athens, GA: Clarke County School District and the University of Georgia.

Malaure, O. (2017, May 8). *Why a good brand is so important to your school's marketing*. [Blog]. The Finalsite Blog. Retrieved from https://www.finalsite.com/blog/p/~post/why-a-good-brand-is-so-important-to-your-schools-marketing-20170509

Moore, P. (2017). *Social media policy & governance: 17 tips to mitigate social business risk*. [Blog]. Saint Cloud, FL: Marketing Nutz. Retrieved from http://www.pammarketingnut.com/2014/05/social-media-policy-governance-17-tips-to-mitigate-social-business-risk/

Notter, J. (n.d.). *How social media is changing leadership*. [Blog]. Retrieved from https://blog.marketo.com/2013/06/how-social-media-is-changing-leadership.html

Parrotte, S. (2017, April 18). *Give your brand a soul: Why vision, mission and values matter*. [Blog]. Goalcast. Retrieved from https://www.goalcast.com/2017/04/18/give-brand-why-soul-vision-mission-values-matter/

Pew Research Center (2017). *Internet/broadband fact sheet*. Washington, DC: Pew Research Center. Retrieved from http://www.pewinternet.org/fact-sheet/internet-broadband/

Sametz, R. (n.d.a). *When change is necessary: Five reasons to embark on re-branding*. Boston, MA: Sametz Blackstone Associates. Retrieved from https://sametz.com/articles/five-reasons-to-rebrand/

Sametz, R. (n.d.b). *When change is unnecessary: Five reasons not to embark on re-branding*. Boston, MA: Sametz Blackstone Associates. Retrieved from https://sametz.com/articles/when-change-is-unnecessary-five-reasons-not-to-embark-on-re-branding/

Smiciklas, M. (2013). Social media transparency [Infographic]. *Social Media Explorer*. Retrieved from https://socialmediaexplorer.com/social-media-marketing/social-media-transparency-infographic/

The Dynamics of Governance

LETTER FROM THE SUPERINTENDENT

Dear Faculty and Staff:

First, thank you for the decisions you make every day to support our students. As you know, our recent strategic plan outlines our intent to develop a charter system application with the state that would give the district greater flexibility in making decisions with a shift from a central governance model to one of local governance at each school. Our goal is to design a school-based governance model to make principled decisions to support the unique needs of every student, school, and our community.

Through a decentralized governance model, members of school communities will be able to innovate by leveraging each school's community assets to support the needs of students, families, faculty and staff, and their communities. Through local decision-making, schools can better identify their needs and leverage their resources to support students in the context of the overall strategic goals of the district.

Over the next six months, we will hold community focus forums in every school in the district to hear perspectives and solicit recommendations as we outline local governance processes and a framework for our charter system application. We will communicate the dates and times of these meetings from the district office, but please use your communication outlets to inform your community of these forums. To ensure transparency, we will provide a summary of these meetings posted on the district's web site.

This process is critical to better serve our communities as we build systems to strengthen our programs for students.

Sincerely,

Superintendent

The conversations around governance may appear straightforward and easily defined through lists that "spell out" the responsibilities of school boards or other governing entities with those of superintendents. However, the dynamics of governance is more than a list and is one of the most challenging responsibilities for superintendents in leading and managing districts. In far too many instances, school boards and their leaders are ineffective because of getting entangled within each other's responsibilities.

Boards go beyond their roles of governance in areas of policy, budget, personnel selection, and the evaluation of the superintendent. Equally problematic is when superintendents make decisions that are contrary to board policy or counter to the positions of the board. Today, the need to understand roles and responsibilities of both the school board and superintendents becomes intensified as districts seek to transform themselves. Superintendents carry the responsibility to engage boards in constructive interactions that lead to the development of policies to define their roles and to model a decision-making framework for governance throughout the district.

However, recent efforts to transform schools by focusing on governance structures have not resulted in desired changes, further illustrating the complexities around governance and decision-making to improve performance. Moreover, decision makers often have a lack of understanding on the impact of governance within the system. This lack of understanding becomes evident as schools and systems make fundamental shifts in the work of the district and its schools to improve the achievement for all children.

As school leaders look for the changes in their systems, historical perspectives provide great insight into why schools have been unable to transform in ways to meet the demands placed on schools. McGuinn and Manna (2013, p. 2) posed a question worth examining: "Who governs schools and with what results?" Their assertion is that very little attention has been given to school governance over the last few decades.

McGuinn and Manna (2013) assert that governance models are "highly fragmented, decentralized, politicized, and bureaucratic and contributes to these problems by undercutting the development and sustenance of changes needed to improve the education opportunities and academic performance of students" (p. 3). Therefore, superintendents now have a primary role in developing effective governance models.

For district and school leaders, navigating the dynamics of governance goes well beyond individual decisions and policies. Successful governance requires clarity at every level related to the roles and responsibilities that contribute to the "purpose" of the school, as defined by its vision, mission, and beliefs. Effective and successful governance models keep the focus on what is important and help to deflect the distractions that occur daily in schools.

Creating a constant focus on the governance within the district allows leaders to develop effective policies to innovate the system and to navigate the noise that the change creates. McGuinn and Manna (2013) offered that leaders must lead in "a larger context by focusing needed attention on the governance forest without getting lost in these policy trees" (p. 3). Essentially, the superintendent will approve the purchase of tires for the bus while the school board develops policies on how to purchase the tires for the bus.

BOARD AND SUPERINTENDENT LEADERSHIP

Superintendents and school boards can easily become distracted from the work that should directly focus on the performance of the district. The distractions include for example, federal and state accountability systems, scrutiny of teachers and school leaders, and the growing role of legislators in education. For superintendents, their primary responsibility is keeping all members of their school boards focused on the direction and performance of the district and their decisions that move system forward. According to Bridges (1982), "the superintendent stands at the apex of the organizational pyramid in education and manages a multi-million dollar enterprise charged with the moral and technical socialization of youth, aged 6–18" (p. 23).

The School Board

While the role of the school board cannot be distilled into a single list, the Center for Public Education (2011) outlines characteristics of effective school boards that have impacted student achievement. School boards are most effective when they embrace these qualities and characteristics that lead to improved performance of the district. These characteristics include:

- Hold a vision of high expectations for student achievement and high-quality instruction, and outline clear, specific goals toward the vision.
- Hold shared beliefs and values about the ability of all students to learn and of the system and its ability to instruct all children at high levels.

- Are driven by accountability and focus more on policies that improve student achievement rather than operational issues.
- Engage in collaborative partnerships with staff and community and a clear structure of communication to inform and engage internal and external stakeholders in establishing student achievement goals for the district.
- Welcome data, whether positive or negative, and use it to drive continuous improvement.
- Align and sustain resources (e.g., professional development) in order to meet goals of the district, even in times of budgetary limitations.
- Lead with the superintendent as a united team, each holding their own roles in the process with strong collaboration and a mutual trust.
- Engage in team development and training, sometimes including superintendents, to build shared knowledge, values, and commitments for improvement efforts. (paras. 2–9)

Maintaining the qualities of effective school boards requires continuous attention. Superintendents and board leaders often ignore or minimize the time needed to assess their effectiveness which ripples throughout the system.

School systems are most effective when roles and responsibilities are clearly understood and enacted. Littleford (2015) emphasizes the need for the school board to be healthy and focused because, "schools with healthy boards do not have crises. They have solutions. Schools with unhealthy boards make small incidents into crises and respond with hysteria rather than wisdom" (para. 1).

The Superintendent

Equally important is for superintendents to reflect on their effectiveness both in working with their boards and in supporting the work described in the strategic plan of the district. In a literature review of effective superintendents, the ECRA Group (2010) established six critical domain areas for superintendents to focus efforts.

1. *Vision and Values*—the districts leader's vision and commitment to excellence; the alignment of district programs to the broader mission, vision, and philosophy of the district; and the promotion and upholding of high expectations for all stakeholders, including his/her own professional behavior.
2. *Core Knowledge and Competencies*—the district leader's subject matter expertise in the various instructional, managerial, legal, financial, and personnel issues superintendents must face and respond to every day.

3. *Instructional Leadership*—the district leader's ability to plan, implement, and evaluate the efficacy of the school or district's instructional and assessment programming as well as to use that data and other sources of external research to inform district improvement practices.
4. *Community and Relationships*—the district leader's ability to involve stakeholders, particularly school personnel and the school board, in realizing the district's vision and improve student achievement.
5. *Communication and Collaboration*—the district leader's performance as the voice of the district, in the way district performance is communicated to the school and to the external community and superintendent, provides feedback to those with whom he/she collaborates.
6. *Management*—the district leader's effectiveness in aligning district systems and operations (e.g., budgeting, compliance) and organizational performance to the goals and values of the district. (p. 5)

The critical aspect of the work of the superintendent is how these areas of focus intersect with the responsibilities of the board. Ultimately, the effectiveness of superintendents may be defined by their leadership in this space.

Expending critical time and energy in keeping the board focused on performance and the elements of the strategic plan must be a priority if the district is going to move forward in educating students. Assessing the level of focus of both the board and the superintendent can help minimize the distractions and even mitigate individual board member agendas. School boards and superintendents become dysfunctional when too much time is wasted due to their inability to understand their roles. Healthy systems have a focus on outcomes for adults and students in the system while unhealthy systems focus on the individual governing members.

Positive Relationships Through Communication

Keeping the board focused on the performance of students and the district requires a relationship built on trust and open communication Accountability is showing no sign of abating, and the push for accountability has created distractions that can lead boards to lose sight of their role, resulting in conflict and resentment between the board and the superintendent. Building relationships and developing trust between the board and the superintendent is mission critical as schools navigate the new challenges of accountability to all students in the district.

For superintendents to maintain a focus on performance, they must establish effective communication streams with the board to lead them in enacting their roles. The effectiveness of governance by the board and superintendent requires an elevated level of transparency that is a responsibility of the superintendent. In the final analysis, effective communication is foundational to effective school board and superintendent governance. The challenge for superintendents is identifying effective communication systems and being patient, given all their other responsibilities in leading and operating the school district.

Power Dynamics Between the Superintendent and the Board

Mountford (2004) reported, "School board members who practice power in a dominating or oppressive manner can overtly and covertly exert influence over school activities in ways that make the decision-making process and relationships between board members and superintendents difficult at best" (p. 704). The conflict is real and determines the success or failure of both the superintendent and the board and their collective ability to focus and to improve student learning. Stressed board relationships have created an instability for superintendents across the country. In a national study, Kowalski, McCord, Peterson, Young, and Ellerson (2011) examined superintendent longevity and found that approximately 15 percent of superintendents leave their positions because of conflict with the board.

Superintendents are placed in a difficult position in their relationship with the board when individual board members work outside of the board as a single entity. The "confusion over roles, most often due to board members overstepping their boundaries by meddling in administrative affairs, can cause inefficiency and conflict" according to Hanover Research (2014, p. 3). It is here where superintendents cannot navigate through these issues alone.

Heads of school boards have a leader responsibility of working with other board members and will need to assume a significant role when board dysfunction gets in the way of effective and healthy governance. For superintendents, the critical decision is deciding at what level this is occurring with board members and when to get the head of the board actively involved. Keeping the focus on district performance and using "student achievement as the primary barometer" will lead to the most productive results in the governance of schools and school districts (Hanover Research, 2014, p. 4).

These conversations send a clear message to the internal and external community of the school board and point to the district leadership's interests and priorities. When the focus of the school community shifts to the interactions between school board and superintendent is when the decisions required to support all children become counter to the work required. In the end, "successful districts require board members to focus on long-term strategic planning and superintendents to focus on successfully implementing policy" (Hanover Research, 2014, p. 3).

Reflecting on the Work
In keeping the focus on performance . . .
1. Are work sessions and school board meetings predominantly about instructional decisions? 2. Is the focus of your board on individual board member issues or on student performance?

SUPPORTING DECISIONS AT EVERY LEVEL

While most superintendents commit their time to the governance of the board, it is paramount that superintendents generate clarity in the decision-making processes throughout the system. Transforming schools to meet the needs of all students requires decision-making and leadership at all levels from those with formal titles (principal, superintendent, etc.) to those who make decisions everyday within the context of their work (e.g., teachers). However, according to Leithwood, Seashore Louis, Anderson, and Wahlstrom (2004) those with formal titles will likely have the greatest influence.

The future success of districts and schools requires a shift in governance to models that are horizontal in their design rather than the conventional vertical model (top down). With this shift, the superintendent's focus should be on a system where the vision, mission, and beliefs are at the center of the system, and leaders within the system understand their varying roles in making aligned and supported short-term and long-range decisions. Allowing systems to create decision-making at every level requires planning with clarity in the work, developing safe cultures with defined responsibilities, and establishing monitoring system for continuous feedback.

A clear vision, mission, and beliefs along with a focused strategic plan are foundational for good decisions to be made at every level across the system. According to Seashore Louis, Leithwood, Wahlstrom, and Anderson (2010), moving away from top-down decision-making models and distributing critical decision-making processes to multiple constituents at the school has shown to produce positive results in moving the needle to improve the learning experiences and achievement for children.

For superintendents, the challenge is to 1) ensure a prominent level of trust has been established to allow decisions to be made at every level of the organization and 2) design systems for monitoring to ensure there is alignment to the strategic plan and district goals set by the school board.

Developing a Trusting Culture for Effective Decision-Making

While it is easy as a superintendent to view distributed leadership by roles and functions of leaders in the system, establishing trust in a culture of distributive decision-making requires attention to individual practices and the interactions of leaders as they seek solutions. According to Spillane (2005), "leadership practice takes form in the interactions between leaders and followers, rather than as a function of one or more leaders' actions" (p. 146).

Inherent in developing a trusting culture where members of the organization feel safe requires a range of freedom and experimentation by letting adults take risks for the good of children. Superintendents or district leaders cannot micromanage; rather, they must empower others to make the decisions necessary by allowing them to create their own working framework. With the freedom to govern and make decisions, those "on the front line" can better navigate the information and needs to find the best solutions. For district leaders, their role becomes more of a supportive one with a "how can I help?" and "what do you need?" type of approach to develop solutions.

Understanding and enacting clear roles for the superintendent and school board is central to the health of the system and for creating an environment where others are empowered to make decisions to impact the system at every level. When the relationship between the board and superintendent is healthy, the system is healthy. When effective decisions are made at every level in the system is when students have the greatest opportunity to grow and succeed.

Reflecting on the Work
In supporting decisions at every level . . . 1. How would those that work with you describe your leadership style? Do you make changes based on their feedback? 2. Is your decision-making model clear enough to give guidance but flexible enough to allow critical decisions at every level?

NAVIGATING THE POLITICAL VOICES

With the No Child Left Behind Act of 2001 and Every Student Succeeds Act of 2015, increasing control of education has been given to federal and state policy-makers. This shift has changed the role of superintendents where they must now navigate new political territory as they lead school transformation requiring extensive networking and continuous conversations because of:

- A newly forming marketplace for schools, evolving systems of account-ability to measure student performance as well as the performance of teachers and leaders.
- The impact of state and federal politics on the community at large, and on district systems.
- Collective bargaining and agreements that outline the working conditions in schools that often maintain traditional school frameworks.
- Privatization of schools and school choice.
- Shifting communities across the country

Collaborating to redefine the work will require leaders in all sectors influencing education to come together in a unique way for the good of all students. Superintendents must be the pivotal leader in navigating the many voices and influences that have an impact on the system.

Work Agreements and Contracts

Historically, school districts that engaged in developing collective agreements and contracts have made significant improvements in the conditions for both teachers and support personnel. Setting the right conditions for the adults has a major impact on the culture of any school or district. If teachers are to achieve success for students, they must rely on a positive and supportive cul-ture in both their schools and their district.

Far too often, the traditions of school immobilize their ability to change. As a result, leading through change becomes tedious and often entangled with adult issues that schools should essentially remain the same. According to Hatch and Hess (2015) "reform-minded school superintendents are now too often constrained by contract provisions and spending arrangements that long predate their leadership, meaning their schools' budgets and staffing decisions are largely shaped by forces beyond their control" (para. 7).

Committed leaders of every working group can find the way to make the needed changes to support new work cultures that have a focus on all students. The process begins by developing trust within the different adult organizations and by identifying common interest where all agree that change needs to occur.

Legislative

It is glaringly obvious that the role of legislators in educational reform has come to prominence in public education. Recently, legislative action in the movements of privatization, public school vouchers, and flow of resources have and will remain mainstream in their impact on the design of public education. According to Thomas (2012), "the faces and voices currently leading the education reform movement in the U.S. are appointees and self-proclaimed reformers who, while often well-meaning, lack significant expertise or experience in education" (para. 7). This dynamic will have the greatest influence on educational policy and will be one of the most significant challenges for superintendents.

Superintendents need to have the courage to stand up and stand out. Superintendents need to have different conversations to change the course for students failing in our school systems. In an interview with Christopher Cross, Lamiell (2012) reports, "If we resolve to educate every child in this country, regardless of ZIP code, we're going to have to dismantle what we're doing. We're not going to get there without significant disruption" (para. 13, emphasis in the original).

Teachers and school leaders make a difference every day. School personnel who excel in perpetuating the bureaucracies that hold change hostage, miss the mark. Thomas (2012) spoke to this point when he cited Philip K. Howard, a legal reformer who stated, "Educators and researchers can lead schools if we will commit ourselves to genuine social reform that addresses poverty, and to education reform that allows teachers to do that which they know how to do" (p. 19).

Community

Community mapping typically begins at the onset of taking office. The starting point is through a well-defined and strategic entry plan that engages internal and external stakeholders. At the onset of taking office, superintendents can begin critical conversations and partnerships that not only signal collaboration, but also signal an awareness of the communities' voices and how they can be leveraged for ongoing collaboration. The caution for superintendents is understanding the balance of time and energy required for outreach while at the same time understanding the inner workings of the system and handling the day-to-day operations.

Balance is needed for superintendents to stay focused on the district while meeting with outside agencies that may feel at times as not central to the work. Scheduling an hour on a regular basis with individual community leaders builds needed trust and knowledge of how other organizations support the school and its children. School districts typically get community support in hiring a superintendent, so it makes great sense for superintendents to include the community in supporting the work of schools.

The Reform Support Network (2014) conducted studies of urban and rural districts engaged in communities with low-performing schools, and they identified five takeaways for developing effective community collaboration, including strategies to:

1. Make engagement a priority and establish an infrastructure. State and district leaders made community engagement a priority and set up an infrastructure to implement that commitment.
2. Communicate proactively in the community. Seeking to engage a community in pending reform, it finds ways to **inform** that community.
3. Listen to the community and respond to its feedback. **Inquire** of their communities—through conversations, public forums, surveys, and focus groups—in order to understand and address local issues and concerns.
4. Offer meaningful opportunities to participate. Meaningful ways to **involve** parents and community members in school improvement and support for student achievement.
5. Turn community supporters into leaders and advocates. Thoughtfully informing, inquiring, and involving families and community representatives, turnaround leaders and staff to **inspire** more of them to share their knowledge and enthusiasm, persuade others and actively campaign for school turnaround. (p. 3, emphasis in the original)

Understanding the political as well as stakeholder voices is about building relationships, staying informed, and understanding how support at all levels politically influences superintendent and school board decisions. Eadie (2009) shared:

> Stakeholder relationships are far too important to your district's welfare to take a catch-as-catch-can approach, or just to rely on squeaky wheels to tell you when you need to pay attention to a particular relationship. The health of these relationships depends on meticulous planning and execution, and detailed board involvement is a must. (p. 43)

The relationships and dynamics of organizations external to the system can create stability and new opportunities that have both short-term and long-term effects. Through positive relationships with internal and external stakeholders, superintendents are able to steer the political voices in a way to lead change and reform as well as to navigate the daily pitfalls that occur in school districts.

Reflecting on the Work
In navigating the political voices . . . 1. Reflect on a situation where the politics of the community stalled a great initiative. Based on what you learned from this experience, what would you do differently to navigate the politics? 2. Identify potential state legislative actions in education that would affect your district and contact your legislators to discuss their positions.

STAYING FOCUSED AMID DISTRACTIONS

In all that is said about the need for positive relationships between the superintendent and school board to establish effective governance, the vulnerability to internal and external distractions may have the most significant impact if not effectively navigated. Today, many boards spend an inordinate amount of time on issue-driven responses to something that happened in the school district, an issue in the community, or an individual board member's personal agenda. Distractions for school boards will likely never go away. However, with clear roles and responsibilities and a commitment to follow governing rules, school boards and superintendents can establish effective governance models that can minimize distractions in a way to keep focused on district priorities.

As superintendents and school boards expand their leadership roles into the community to serve children better, the number and kinds of distractions will increase, causing significant stress on the board's ability to make effective decisions. In addition, some elected school board members might not be prepared to engage in their roles while some members have their own agendas derived from their election platforms.

According to Reimer (2015), "school boards will struggle with their mandates because the people who are confused with their roles are elected, and the multiple other influences on school board governance offer compelling distractions" (p. 15). Boards need to have a strong focus on assessing their governance effectiveness and strategies for improvement. Without this focus, boards will fail their systems and the work that they have been entrusted to do on behalf of their communities.

Internal School Board Distractions

One the quickest tests to determine if the board is functioning as one may be the headlines in the local media or social media outlets. If the headlines continue to focus on the workings of the school board and superintendent, there is a great likelihood that the board is not focused on the work but rather they are consumed by distractions. When this happens, school boards lose their credibility within the system and the community.

When boards lose their credibility, this creates an even greater level of vulnerability chipping away at their effectiveness. Most likely, boards have this internal dysfunction when they are not clear about their roles and responsibilities, or in many cases, when one or more board members choose to work from their own agenda and not from the agenda of the board as a whole. Stover (2011) describes the challenge of most boards like this:

> Call it what you will: Boards micromanage. They allow themselves to be distracted by day-to-day operational issues. They react to every community complaint. They get down in the weeds instead of soaring at 30,000 feet, where they belong. (p. 4)

It is essential that superintendents are aware of potential problems and work directly to seek resolution before these issues escalate.

Creating policy and protocols to keep the board away from distractions by clarifying how issues come to the board and who manages them will minimize the noise that often distracts them. Once policies are developed, it becomes the boards' ultimate responsibility to follow them. We know that issues should be resolved at their closest point and by those who are directly responsible; that is not at the board level. If superintendents can effectively lead, boards will significantly increase the time they need to focus on the performance of the district.

System Distractions

Superintendents play a pivotal role in supporting a culture of risk-taking and innovation to improve performance. Often, change creates a culture tagged mistakenly as one of "low morale" by those in the system that are recalcitrant to doing things differently. Having systems in place to counter the veneer of "low morale" diverts the attention on the most pressing issues that need to be addressed as the system is undergoing transformation. If the health of the district culture is not understood, the discontent will quickly get to the board level and cause significant distractions from the new work that is needed.

While much has been written about the health of school cultures and teacher morale, for the purpose here regarding board distractions, it is central that superintendents determine structures to empower teachers and school leaders to make decisions at the school level and put in place protocols to hear constructive feedback on school programs. The balance is to delineate between the individual's dissatisfaction with the work by examining constructive feedback for school and district improvement.

The pressure often mounts when those in the system go above those closest to handling the situation that frequently leads directly to board members. Protocols for board involvement are paramount in a system so that the superintendent can react and respond to complaints within the system using consistent procedures. When effective protocols are in place and followed, the board is freed from not only distractions but also from moving away from their role in the governance of the district.

External Distractions

When superintendents are asked to present a list about possible community distractions, the response would likely be, "There is a running list." Each community has a unique interplay with their school district. Superintendents can take advantage of distractions to create change while others create change through strategic planning. In either scenario, superintendents need to understand the impact of distractions that can occur as change is being enacted. Moreover, superintendents need to know where the distractions originate in their community. Superintendents cannot afford to be blindsided with negative distractions that can escalate.

Superintendents cannot always know what crisis could move the attention away from governing the district. With constantly growing social media platforms, community distractions can be amplified, and even manufactured, with crisis-level fallout before the superintendent is aware that there is a problem. Interestingly, superintendents who are viewed as traditional typically focus and handle distractions from outside the system well, whereas more nontraditional superintendents typically focus on learning and instruction and get more annoyed with anything that gets in the way (Fuller et al., 2003).

Reflecting on the Work
In staying focused amid distractions . . . 1. How do you work with individual board members who are working outside of their defined responsibilities? 2. To support healthy cultures of change and innovation, have you developed a feedback mechanism internal to the system?

SUMMARY

School governance is complex. There are opinions that school governance is effective because it reflects the core of democracy while others say it is dysfunctional in moving school districts forward due to personal board member agendas. However, district governance is at its best when the superintendent and board understand the impact of a positive working relationship and a collective focus on district priorities. Ultimately the district will either grow and prosper or function in disarray depending on the leadership at this level.

The work and daily grind can take a toll on superintendents both professionally and personally. In chapter 8, sitting and former superintendents from around the country provide their insights and perspectives on the balance needed to be successful and healthy in their professional and personal lives.

A SUPERINTENDENT'S DIVE INTO LEADING THE DYNAMICS OF GOVERNANCE

1. Review your board and superintendent self-assessment for governance. Develop a plan for improvement around the five central characteristics of effective school board and superintendent relationships.
2. Review your current feedback systems and assess their effectiveness in influencing changes to policies, protocols, and practices.
3. As a leader, how do you engage the community in giving input on board decisions?

SUGGESTED READINGS

Hirsh, S., & Foster, A. (2013). *A school board guide to leading successful schools: Focusing on learning.* Thousand Oaks, CA: Corwin Press.

Reimer, L. E. (2015). *Leadership and school boards: Guarding the trust in an era of community engagement* (2nd ed.). Lanham, MD: Rowman & Littlefield.

White, P. C., Harvey, T. R., & Fox, S. L. (2016). The politically intelligent leader: Dealing with the dilemmas of a high-stakes educational environment (2nd ed.). Lanham, MD: Rowman & Littlefield.

REFERENCES

Bridges, E. M. (1982). Research on the school administrator: The state of the art, 1967–1980. *Educational Administration Quarterly, 18*(3), 12–33. doi: 10.1177/00 13161X82018003003

Center for Public Education. (2011). *Eight characteristics of effective school boards: At a glance.* Alexandria, VA: Center for Public Education. Retrieved from http://www.centerforpubliceducation.org/Main-Menu/Public-education/ Eight-characteristics-of-effective-school-boards

Eadie, D. (2009). High stakes strategy: Bringing outside groups to the board table. *American School Board Journal, 1,* 43–44. Retrieved from http://www.asbj.com/

ECRA Group. (2010). *Effective superintendents: ECRA literature review.* Rosemont, IL: ECRA Group, Inc. Retrieved from http://resources.aasa.org/ConferenceDaily/ handouts2011/3000-1.pdf

Every Student Succeeds Act. (2015). Pub. L. 114-95, 129 Stat. 1802.

Fuller, H. L., Campbell, C., Celio, M. B., Harvey, J., Immerwahr, J., & Winger, A. (2003). *An impossible job? The view from the urban superintendent's chair.* Seattle, WA: University of Washington. Center on Reinventing Public Education. Retrieved from https://crpe.org/sites/default/files/pub_crpe_imposs_jul03_0.pdf

Hanover Research. (2014). *Effective board and superintendent collaboration.* Washington, DC: Hanover Research. Retrieved from http://www.hanoverresearch. com/wp-content/uploads/2014/08/Effective-Board-and-Superintendent-Collaboration.pdf

Hatch, O., & Hess, F. M. (2015, July 16). Let's give schools the flexibility they need to achieve real reform. [Blog]. National Review. Retrieved from http:// www.nationalreview.com/article/421248/lets-give-schools-flexibility-they-need-achieve-real-reform-orrin-hatch-frederick-m

Kowalski, T. J., McCord, R. S., Peterson, G. J., Young, I. P., & Ellerson, N. M. (2011). *The American school superintendent: 2010 decennial study.* Arlington, VA: American Association of School Administrators.

Lamiell, P. (2012). *How should politics influence education policy?* Teacher College Newsroom. New York, NY: Teachers College, Columbia University. Retrieved from http://www.tc.columbia.edu/articles/2012/february/ how-should-politics-influence-education-policy/

Leithwood, K., Louis, K. S., Anderson, S. E., & Wahlstrom, K. L. (2004). *How leadership influences student learning: A review of research for the Learning from Leadership Project.* New York, NY : The Wallace Foundation.

Littleford, J. (2015). Evaluation of boards: Self-reflection in a healthy school. Baton Rouge, LA: Littleford & Associates. Retrieved from http://www.jlittleford.com/ evaluation-of-boards-self-reflection-in-a-healthy-school/

McGuinn, P., & Manna, P. (2013). Education governance in America: Who leads when everyone is in charge? In P. Manna & P. McGuinn (Eds.). *Educational governance for the twenty-first century: Overcoming the structural barriers to school reform* (pp. 1–17). Washington, DC: Thomas B. Fordham Institute, Center for American Progress, & Brookings Institute Press. Retrieved from https://www.brookings.edu/wpcontent/uploads/2016/07/educationgovernance_chapter.pdf

Mountford, M. (2004). Motives and power of school board members: Implications for school board-superintendent relationships. *Educational Administration Quarterly, 40*(5), 704–741. doi: 10.1177/0013161X04268843

No Child Left Behind Act. (2001). Pub. L. 107-10, 115 Stat. 1425, as amended by 20 U.S.C. § 6301 (2015).

Reform Support Network. (2014). *Strategies for community engagement in school turnaround*. Washington, DC: U.S. Department of Education. Retrieved from https://www2.ed.gov/about/inits/ed/implementation-support-unit/tech-assist/strategies-for-community-engagement-in-school-turnaround.pdf

Reimer, L. E. (2015). *Leadership and school boards: Guarding the trust in an era of community engagement* (2nd ed.). Lanham, MD: Rowman & Littlefield.

Seashore L. K., Leithwood, K., Wahlstrom, K. L, & Anderson, S. E. (2010). *Investigating the links to improved student learning: Final report of research findings from the learning from leadership project*. New York, NY: The Wallace Foundation. Retrieved from http://www.wallacefoundation.org/knowledge-center/Documents/Investigating-the-Links-to-Improved-Student-Learning.pdf

Spillane, J. P. (2005). Distributed leadership. *The Educational Forum, 69*(2), 143–150, doi: 10.1080/00131720508984678

Stover, D. (2011, January 5). How to avoid operational distractions. [Blog]. *American School Board Journal*. Retrieved from http://www.asbj.com/TopicsArchive/Leadership/How-to-Avoid-Operational-Distractions.html

Thomas, P. L. (2012, April 26). Politics and education don't mix. [Blog]. *The Atlantic*. Retrieved from https://www.theatlantic.com/national/archive/2012/04/politics-and-education-dont-mix/256303/

Chapter 8

Your Balance Is the System's Balance

IN THIS CHAPTER ...

- The Public Eye
- The Never Ending Work
- The Work Is Personal
- Work and Family Balance
- Sleeping at Night

LETTER FROM THE SUPERINTENDENT

Dear Sylvia:

I thoroughly enjoyed our meeting yesterday and having an opportunity to share some insights into the work of the superintendent. It was not that long ago when I was in the identical position you are in now, exploring opportunities for becoming a superintendent. There have been many lessons learned during my years as a teacher, principal, and superintendent. However, the most important and most difficult lesson for me has been keeping a physical and emotional balance between leading in my school district and community and spending time with my family and personal interests.

Keeping a focus on your family seems most obvious and the easiest, but it is not. The 24-7 nature of the job of superintendent pulls at your attention. The calls during those off times when you are at a family gathering can take its toll. The times that you try to balance between a family and a school event can tear you apart. In the end, it is your family that remembers only too well how you had to check out during birthday parties for the grandchildren, the surprise party for your wife, and even on the holiday carving of the Thanksgiving turkey.

The times you were there with family but not there in your mind because you were concerned about an issue results in lost time you cannot get back. Your family knows when you are present and when you are not, so it is important to be able to turn off the work or turn it over to someone else. We talk about family as being the most important priority, but if you do not put in place safeguards, in practice, your family can slip to background status.

Working within your own philosophical beliefs appears to be an easy task because you always try to stay within yourself. However, being a superintendent is as much about understanding the beliefs held by those in your system and your community as it is about your own understanding. Understanding the multiple perspectives will help you in making very difficult decisions based on varying principles. When you wake up at three o'clock in the morning thinking about an issue or a problem, try to go back to sleep— you will have many sleepless nights. Staying awake thinking about an issue does not usually bring clarity.

The workload is intense for sure, but so is being a school leader or a teacher. The work will always be there in the morning, so just understand that. You cannot get it all done. To start the day with new work—this is not a reality for a superintendent. Almost every day will be filled with yesterday's work. Know that in the end, everything can be accomplished if you prioritize your time. I strongly suggest that you keep yourself in good physical health and that means time for yourself. A good night's sleep or some exercise goes a long way.

What is it like being a superintendent? I say it is the best job in the world. You have an opportunity to set the bar to new heights for many children. You have an opportunity to create a culture where adults are appreciated and love coming to work even in stressful environments created by high-stakes testing, ever rising accountability bars, and the ungrateful public naysayers. You have an opportunity to make decisions for not only what happens tomorrow but also for what happens one to ten years out. You have an opportunity to create and lead healthy communities. Finally, being a superintendent is an opportunity for you to become a better person—it did for me.

Sylvia, my last thoughts about this journey are for you to think about who you are and what you want to become known for as a leader. I believe the superintendency is right for you.

Sincerely,

Superintendent

Attempting to find balance between the work in one's professional life and one's personal life is not a new concept. There are some that espouse there will never be balance between work and personal life. One of the most significant challenges for superintendents is finding the balance with the public nature of the work required with their personal and family life. Knowing that the boundaries between work and family are not clear, superintendents try creating "compartments" to help separate and organize life. This is easier said than done.

While superintendents across the country share much in common with their responsibilities, each brings their own perspectives on their journey. Chapter 8 is unique in that successful sitting and former superintendents share their reflections about how they were able to navigate "the balance." In responding to key questions, they share reflections about balancing their lives in the public eye with the personal needs of their families, and the challenges of unifying the multitude of philosophies in their communities with their own beliefs about educating all students.

You will read the perspectives from a celebrated cadre of leaders that include:

- Dr. Peter I. Burrows, superintendent of the Addison Central School District (Middlebury, Vermont), has served in education for 25 years as a teacher, principal, and superintendent. Prior to entering administration, Dr. Burrows spent 15 years as a Teacher of English as a Second Language and a high school Language Arts teacher both nationally and internationally. Dr. Burrows's greatest satisfaction in the work of educational leadership is the students and parents who come back to share how their lives have changed through their educational experiences.
- Mr. Dennis W. Dearden, president and cofounder of Monkey Business Associates, LLC (Oro Valley, Arizona), is a former superintendent and associate superintendent. Dr. Dearden also served as the associate executive director with AASA, The School Superintendents Association. Serving in education for 42 years, Mr. Dearden has fulfilled such roles as teacher, coach, and principal.
- Dr. Susan Enfield, superintendent of the Highline Public Schools (Burien, Washington), has served as a central office leader, a school improvement coach, and a high school English and journalism teacher. Dr. Enfield served education at the state level. Of all her accolades, none mean more to her than being recognized by former students who, upon reaching college, have nominated her as the Most Influential Teacher at the University of California, Santa Barbara (2000, 1997), University of Arizona (1997), College of Wooster (1996), Carleton College (1995), and Tufts University (1994). Dr. Enfield is celebrating her 25th year in education.
- Dr. Sybil Knight-Burney, superintendent of the Harrisburg School District (Harrisburg, Pennsylvania), previously served as an assistant

superintendent, a high school principal, and elementary and middle school principal as well as an assistant principal at these levels. At the executive level, Dr. Knight-Burney served as a district coordinator of Educational Equity & Student Reassignment & Choice Specialist and as an Assistant Director to plan and open the Cypress Lake Center for the Arts. Dr. Knight-Burney received the Golden Apple Teacher Award in Fort Myers, Florida, for excellence in teaching. She brings 36 years of service to education.

- Dr. Patrice Pujol is president of the National Institute for Excellence in Teaching (Baton Rouge, Louisiana), a major nonprofit. Prior to that, she served as a superintendent, an assistant superintendent, a district level director, a high school principal and assistant principal, and an English teacher, totaling 41 years in public education. Dr. Pujol was one of four semifinalists for the 2015 National Superintendent of the Year recognition by the American Association of School Administrators.
- Dr. Grant Rivera, superintendent of the Marietta City Schools (Marietta, Georgia), has served as a district chief of staff, a high school principal, an assistant principal, and a special education teacher. Throughout his 18 years in education, Dr. Rivera shares that his most important contribution to education is ensuring that students can be successful.
- Dr. Thomas S. Woods-Tucker, superintendent of the Princeton City School District (Cincinnati, Ohio), previously served as a Middle School English and reading teacher, an administrative assistant in nursing and medicine and adjunct professor at the Ohio State University, and a district leader. The most meaningful recognition for Dr. Woods-Tucker occurred in 1989 when 150 seventh and eighth grade girls and boys in Jardine Middle School in Topeka, Kansas, called him, "Teacher!" He brings 20 years of service to education, and in 2016, Dr. Woods-Tucker was named the National Superintendent of the Year by the American Association of School Administrators.

THE PUBLIC EYE

Superintendents are in the public eye every minute of every day and both their personal as well as their professional lives are always on display. Superintendents have intense pressure, not only to be in the public eye, but also to live in the public eye, with requirements or expectations for them to live in the community in which they work. The health and transparency of superintendents are greatly impacted by their ability to manage their visibility within their schools and community, and their ability to create their own personal space.

Dr. Patrice Pujol believes time away from work is not always your own, and the constant barrage from the public can be exhausting. However, meeting with the public provides a human aspect of who you are and that you have something in common. Dr. Pujol reminds us about the nature of being in the public eye.

One of the most demanding aspects of being a superintendent is that you are always expected to be on . . . on stage, on message, on point, on the job. Whether you are at the grocery store, at church, at the bank, or at your granddaughter's softball tournament; if you are in your community, you are likely going to have stakeholders approaching you with problems, complaints, or sometimes just conversation. Regardless, your time even away from work is rarely your own. While this constant barrage can be exhausting, it is also an opportunity to show the real human aspect of who you are in a setting where you at least have some commonality with the person you are talking to.

I have made many a constituents feel valued and comfortable at the softball park in ways that may not have been as easy in my office, and for years after they would ask me how my granddaughter's softball game was progressing. Even if you can't solve the person's problem in that moment, you can connect with them in a personal way that is different than if you were at work.

That being said, you still need to find ways to compartmentalize your life to create some life-work balance or you will never survive the job. One thing that I think is important is to find some interests that take you away from places you will easily be recognized and accessed. My husband, Tim, and I love to boat on the weekends. Out on the water with a group of friends, I am able to recharge and have life be about something other than the superintendency for a few hours. We also enjoy traveling. Again, when we are out exploring new places and seeing new sights, we are not likely to run into people who know me as a superintendent and are more able to enjoy our common interests and decompress from the rigors of the job.

Short weekend trips or even an evening out in an adjoining city can do wonders for freeing your mind from the day to day worries of the job. These types of getaways, however, are only effective if you indeed get away; that is, you allow yourself the freedom to not think about work and the myriad responsibilities and task lists that encompass it. You have to find ways to really live in the moment when you are away from the job, find pleasure in the time you have away. It is only through this kind of mindfulness of the moment at hand that you can restore yourself to a point of being effective when you do return to the crazy demands of the job.

Regardless of the day-to-day every minute on stage, Dr. Pujol believes you can exert some control over your personal life if you make the choice. Superintendents, like Dr. Pujol personalize their responsibility to hear from and find solutions to problems for members of the community.

Dr. Peter Burrows seeks to have the highest level of comfort in his work and as a member of the community. He also shares the need to find personal space amid the constant contact within his community. Finding personal space requires thoughtfulness and intention. Dr. Burrows elaborates on his thoughts about being in the public eye.

I think that superintendents learn quickly that the requirements of the position require significant thoughtfulness and intention to maintain balance between personal and professional. Living in the district in which I am superintendent has made it important for me to both be comfortable being "on" 24-7 in our community, as well as finding time to recharge.

I've found that exercise, time with family, and unstructured time have all been critical.

Perhaps the most important understanding I've developed is that a quest for balance in the position between work and personal life creates continual tension and a quest for a reality that doesn't exist. I've found that embracing the challenges of the position by focusing more on my internal response to the dizzying number of items to accomplish in a day has allowed me to be more effective as a leader and present throughout the day.

Dr. Burrows understands that balancing his life as a public figure will always have tensions and that balance between both personal and professional roles may not exist. He looks within himself and his internal responses in embracing the challenges of a job that is public.

Dr. Susan Enfield sees her work as one of a public figure and with this role comes a level of awareness and responsibility. However, even as a member of her community, she believes her time at home is respected by her community. Dr. Enfield elaborates her thoughts about being in the public eye.

I believe strongly that, whenever possible, superintendents should live in the communities they lead. Being a part of the community you serve not only signals a long-term commitment but it also gives you far more credibility when it comes time to run bonds and levies. Personally, I would have a difficult time asking my neighbors to raise their taxes for our schools while not asking the same of myself.

That said, living within your district can sometimes feel like living under a microscope. I am fortunate that people in my community are very respectful of my time and not at all intrusive—but I know this is not always the case. I am also fortunate to work for a school board who fully supports and encourages me to take time for myself and has realistic expectations for which public events I attend.

Even under the best of circumstances, however, superintendents are still public figures and often very visible members of the community. With this comes a level of awareness and responsibility when attending school events, or even when dining out alone or with family. I have learned that if I am too tired to engage pleasantly with people, I stay home. The last thing any superintendent needs is to be approached by a district staff member or parent and be perceived as aloof or disrespectful—when the truth was that you were really just exhausted. When we can prevent perception from becoming reality, we must.

Having board support and understanding of the superintendent's balance while in the public eye is important for Dr. Enfield, and she knows that staying home or taking personal time is critical especially when she is simply too tired to be pleasant. Dr. Enfield embraces the influence by her ability to stand up for her community because she is a member of the community.

By reflecting on her experiences as an elementary student in her hometown in Florida, Dr. Sybil Burney-Knight draws meaning to her work in the public and her daily actions. She knows firsthand the devastation of inequity, which deepens her drive to be engaged in both her public and personal life. Dr. Burney-Knight elaborates on her thoughts about being in the public eye.

My personal and professional lives first crossed paths beginning in the third grade. I was 8 years old and 1 of 10 children used to integrate schools due to a court order to desegregate my district in my Florida hometown. Each day I boarded a bus to take a 45-minute ride from my safe and comfortable surroundings to another school where my safety was questionable. This and future experiences with inequity and its devastating impact on communities shaped my personal life and career in education. Though it's hard for me to separate the two at times, my personal life deepens the meaning of my daily decisions and actions at work.

Creating my space between personal and professional life is an acquired peace of mind and feeling of satisfaction. Every morning when I awake in the early hours, before I brush my teeth or have a cup of coffee, I begin my day by thanking God for my opportunity to lead my district as the Superintendent and humbled to have been chosen to do this work. This devotional time helps to set the tone of my day. Throughout the day, when I see children smiling and engaged, teachers celebrating their students' achievement, or parents thanking their principals, I feel satisfaction.

When I see students helping other students by hosting a food or toy drive, holding fundraisers, or cheering on students competing in the Special Olympics, I feel satisfaction. Watching teachers work together and coach each other to be better teachers or custodians planning ways to improve the school's environment, I feel satisfaction. When 167 grandparents are celebrated at a school luncheon or other community partners volunteer to help students, I feel satisfaction. Thus, my space is created and carries me through to the next day.

Seeing the success of others carries Dr. Burney-Knight in her efforts to balance her personal life when continually being in the public eye.

Burney-Knight feels blessed to have the opportunity to draw lessons from her work to deepen her personal satisfaction for what she does personally and professionally every day for her students and community.

Takeaways

- The superintendent's role and work can potentially overshadow their personal lives.
- The superintendent's role with the public originates from a personal orientation shaped by the person's beliefs and experiences.
- The superintendent must be intentional with personal time.

Reflecting on the Work
Your balance is the system's balance . . .
1. How do you manage your personal and professional life while in the public's eye?

THE NEVER ENDING WORK

The work of the superintendent never ends. Like most leaders, just when you think you may be caught up with the work, you are soon days behind. While there are many different ways to manage the workload, for superintendents there is always a pile of papers on the corner of the desk and an inbox of emails requiring decisions and a response.

Dr. Susan Enfield describes the importance of managing time to complete the work even to the point of scheduling time to complete the laundry at home. Dr. Enfield speaks to the never ending work of the superintendent.

As a superintendent, the work is never done. Since there is always more to do, the best we can do is be smart and strategic in how we manage our time and lives, personal and professional. I learned this lesson early in the Harvard Superintendents Program, which was incredibly demanding—and part of that demand was learning how to manage my time. I remember fellow students asking me how I made time for everything in my life, and they would sometimes laugh when I showed them my calendar that included time set aside for everything from schoolwork to exercise to laundry.

Laundry, they would ask? And I would reply that if you don't plan out your week, each week, you will find yourself quickly out of clothes at an inopportune moment. While this may sound silly and perhaps mundane, it has served me well as a superintendent.

Dr. Enfield provides a clear message that a superintendent's time is managed when it is planned and not left to chance. She asserts that managing time to get the work done requires the superintendent to be smart and strategic.

Dr. Patrice Pujol also contends that success is knowing what is important and making sure which priorities can be delegated. Dr. Pujol elaborates on her thoughts about the never ending work of the superintendent.

> The superintendency is an unbelievably demanding job. There are more demands on your time than there are hours in the day and you may not be able to get it all done. The key to success is getting done those things that are most critical and having the discernment to know what those things are. As a superintendent the most valuable resource you have is your time. When you consider this fact, the strategic use of your time becomes an absolute.
>
> One of the most important factors in getting everything accomplished is surrounding yourself with a team of talent in whom you have absolute trust. Building on the strengths of the team, you have to determine what to delegate to whom. Delegation is difficult for most leaders, but it is essential. The key is to determine which events, interactions, projects, and tasks absolutely must be done by you or with your strong guidance and which things can be delegated with strategic follow up.
>
> Sometimes superintendents get the false idea that if something is urgent it requires their personal attention. Many things that will cross your desk are extremely urgent, but are they all mission critical? If something is urgent, but not mission critical, it can probably be delegated. Also, many long-term projects or initiatives will need to be delegated. You as the superintendent cannot be the expert in all things, but you need to know who your experts are. One thing to remember, you certainly will delegate projects and tasks to team members, but you cannot completely delegate responsibility for them.
>
> Successful superintendents set up strong processes for checking in with team members to assure they are making appropriate progress and that they have the resources they need for success. Sometimes team members just need affirmation that they are on track; other times they need you to help them problem-solve. Regardless, it is important to remember that ultimately your team's success is your success, so set them up accordingly.

Dr. Pujol ensures she has a talented staff who has the expertise to handle decisions and projects throughout the system. While superintendents may not be the experts, they set up strong processes to monitor and assess the work throughout the system.

Mr. Denny Dearden maintains that superintendents cannot be in the weeds of decision-making but rather must see the big picture. Mr. Dearden elaborates on his thoughts about the never ending work of the superintendent.

Knowing that you are never going to get it all done is the first step. You must prioritize and get the critical things done first. You must learn to delegate to staff that you can trust and then allow them to do their work. If you are always in the weeds with your staff, you will never see the big picture and have the political savvy that it takes to be a great superintendent. It can be very easy for a superintendent to quickly become submerged in the various tasks required to be successful.

It is critical that clear limits be set regarding management of time, schedules, personal commitments, and technology use. You as the district leader will need to set these limits and be disciplined to maintain the guidelines you determine. Intentionally setting guidelines are crucial to maintaining life/work balance.

An effective superintendent has a clear vision and executes it with a laser-like focus. Don't be over ambitious and set too many goals or priorities. It is more important that you focus on continually moving forward. It will help you prioritize and stay focused and not get ahead of yourself.

Mr. Dearden contends that superintendents must set clear boundaries on their time through effective delegation of responsibilities. He also points to the ability of great superintendents to be disciplined around self-imposed guidelines.

Takeaways

- Superintendents understand the value of hiring staff with a high level of expertise so they can effectively delegate responsibilities.
- Superintendents know they must first understand what is most important in the district and make it a priority.
- Superintendents communicate priorities and then intentionally plan their time.

Reflecting on the Work
Your balance is the system's balance . . .
1. How do you get all the work done?

THE WORK IS PERSONAL

For superintendents, influencing the lives of children is as much personal as professional. Superintendents often feel powerless because many variables that impact decisions are not in their control. However, superintendents have an inner drive to create learning opportunities so all students can learn. For this reason, superintendents continually struggle with the personal nature of their work.

Drawing from experiences from his family, Dr. Thomas Woods-Tucker goes directly to the heart of the matter. He sees education as the way to move all students to a better future. Dr. Woods-Tucker reflects about the personal nature of the work of superintendents.

> This calling or this mission-driven work is personal because I learned at a very early age that poverty and education are inextricably linked. In fact, my family exemplifies that education can be the spark able to launch families and communities out of the proverbial cycle of poverty.
>
> My grandparents, Fred and Magnolia Campbell, when they were not preaching the Gospel, taught other sharecroppers how to read, write, calculate their personal debt, and even market their crops during the era of "Jim Crow."
>
> During the late 1980s, I had a front-row seat watching too many pregnant 7th- and 8th-grade girls drop out of school in my hometown of Cotton Plant, Arizona for life on a former plantation. This relegated them into 2nd-class status without literacy skills and mathematics to successfully lead their respective households. The great Common School provided me the power to dream of a better future and the confidence to pursue a higher education, which in turn has motivated subsequent generations of Tuckers.

Dr. Woods-Tucker brings clarity to why education is critical in this country through his own personal picture and conviction that schools must assure the success for all children. He has a personal conviction that education is the spark that launches families out of the poverty cycle.

On most days, Dr. Susan Enfield loves her job but every single day she loves her work. Working with children, families, and community are her personal centering points. Dr. Enfield reflects about the personal nature of the work of superintendents.

> People often ask me if I love my job, and I tell them that most days I love the job, but every single day I love the work. And this is an important distinction because the work of serving children, families and community is truly a joy and a privilege. In fact, I tell people it is a gift. The job, however, is political, demanding and sometimes toxic; we endure that for the sake of the work.
>
> As much as I try to always remember this, I, like every superintendent, have hard days, so when I need a reminder of what is truly important and regain my perspective I visit a kindergarten classroom. There is no better tonic for what ails you as a superintendent than being inspired by the brilliance, energy and optimism of a five-year-old.

Dr. Enfield does not let herself become distracted from the work due to the demands and toxicity of political stress. When she gets close to a point of frustration, she visits schools, which quickly reminds her of the purpose of the superintendent's work.

Mr. Dennis Dearden also goes back to his experiences growing up and vividly describes how a precious moment can make a lifelong difference for a child as it did for him. Mr. Dearden elaborates his thoughts about the personal nature of the work of superintendents.

> I grew up in poverty in an abusive dysfunctional family. I had a fourth-grade teacher come up to me on the playground one day when I was isolating myself because I smelled, and my clothes were dirty. He tapped me on the shoulder and pointed to all the kids playing and said, "Dennis, those kids will be yours someday." I looked up and asked, "What do you mean?"
>
> He replied, "You will be a teacher someday and you will have the responsibility to make sure that all of your students learn every day." Then he turned and pointed to the school and said, "Dennis, someday that building will be yours, and you will be responsible for all the teachers. You will make sure that every student has a teacher who cares and makes them learn each day." He smiled and walked away. It was that day I made the decision to be an educator. Yes, it has been personal for me. I have spent the past 42 years enjoying every moment that I had making a difference in the lives of kids.

Mr. Dearden reminds us that one moment in a child's educational experience can be the moment that is not only remembered but becomes the drive for their success. His one experience has made his 42 years in education that important—it is personal.

Dr. Knight-Burney understands from her work as a teacher how every gesture, comment, and action of a teacher can influence children. Her work as a superintendent is more intense as she has the responsibility of ensuring that every action in schools has a positive impact. Dr. Knight-Burney elaborates her thoughts about the personal nature of the work of superintendents.

> When I began teaching full time in an inner city high school in Miami, Florida, I realized that I had the power to open doors and windows of opportunity for my students. At the same time, I also recognized that, by the wrong hand gesture, facial expression or voice inflection, I could also close doors and create barriers to learning. I knew that I had a limited opportunity and I didn't want to blow it. I took my job so personally that I would get to work every morning around 6:00 am and leave around 9:30 or 10:00 pm every night.
>
> I lived to make every moment a teachable moment. I started to notice that there was a change in my pay and questioned the school's accountant. I found out that the Night School Principal saw me every evening and was convinced that I was teaching classes and was paying me. He couldn't believe that a

teacher would be there late at night if they weren't teaching a night class! So, of course, I started teaching night classes.

Even though I'm not in any particular classroom—my commitment is even more intense. My focus even more clear. And my determination to ensure equity for my inner city students more defined. I've heard so many stories from former students and some adults—all focused on what a teacher said or didn't say that made them dislike or dropout of school. I didn't want to be that kind of teacher. I believed then as I believe now that I want and need for my students to know that they can accomplish great things if they are willing to be committed to their own learning, focused on achieving their goals and persevering.

Through my own planning and preparation, I wanted them to see me as a living example of what you can achieve. As an African American woman and a Superintendent, I know that just my presence sends a strong message throughout my community. I want that message to be positive. I strive to be a positive example and constantly understand the responsibility and influence I can make. I want my message to be: "You, too can do and be in this job!" I never take this work or my position for granted—it's very personal to me.

For Dr. Knight-Burney, being a role model sends a clear message throughout her community. She sees how education can change lives and how hard work and commitment moves children and adults closer to meeting their goals. The work is personal and should never be taken for granted.

Dr. Grant Rivera understands the impact of education on students' lives as he talks with former students. He understands how education not only impact students but how it impacts their families. Dr. Rivera elaborates his thoughts about the personal nature of the work of superintendents.

It is extremely simple . . . the work is personal because you are impacting the lives of children. We empower the hopes and dreams of children today and, equally as important, as adults living a future that we may never see. One of the greatest joys of my day is when I run into a former student. After sharing a special memory or two, I always inquire about their current work or family circumstances. I take pride in knowing that I'm a line or two in their story of success.

My brother is a commercial law attorney at a large, well respected law firm in Atlanta. He lives in a world of multi-million dollar real estate transactions every day. He often says that I have more meaningful, personal interactions by noon on any given day than he has during an entire month of flipping through legal documents. We, as educational leaders, have the humble honor of being invited into intimate, vulnerable moments for children and their families—it's a gentle reminder that this work is very personal.

While the work is challenging, Dr. Rivera is humbled by the opportunity to be a leader who has a door into the personal and intimate nature of how school's impact children and their families. He understands how the interactions in schools on any given day influences their path.

Takeaways

- Superintendents see their work shaped by their own experiences growing up.
- Superintendents understand that every interaction and decision in a school has an impact on children and their families.
- Superintendents understand how education changes life's paths.

Reflecting on the Work

Your balance is the system's balance . . .

1. In what ways is the work personal to you?

WORK AND FAMILY BALANCE

Being a superintendent can place much strain on family life. The personal and family decisions that are private typically are not private for superintendents. The roles superintendents fill are always up for public review, and this responsibility can take a toll on family life. When you add the physical and emotional efforts superintendents dedicate to their work, very little room is left for their families.

Dr. Peter Burrows understands that you need to be 100 percent there when you dedicate family time. Dr. Burrows elaborates on the balance of work and family.

> I've found that it's more important to be fully present in the limited time I do have with my family as opposed to trying to find more time where it often doesn't exist. For me, this means not spending time on my cell phone and continuing the workday through the evening and drifting in and out of conversations with my family because I'm half home and half at work. I do catch up on email after my children go to bed, and make sure that I'm not too obsessed with every text and email sound that chirps from my devices.

Ensuring he does not use family time to respond to emails is a priority for Dr. Burrows. When you are with family, you must be all-in, requiring you to keep work at alternate times in the evening or on weekends—you cannot be half in and half out.

In Dr. Rivera's view, he has seen many educators who are very successful in their work at school but less successful in their role as a parent. Dr. Rivera elaborates on the balance of work and family.

> This one is hard. I've seen far too many educational leaders be more successful at work than they are at home. I don't want to become another statistic, whereby my family struggles because I spend more time with someone else's children. To find better balance between home and work, I give myself (and my assistant) permission to say no. I do not have to be at every event shaking every hand; sometimes it is simply more important for me to be home for dinner reaching for my child's hand to say the blessing.

There comes a time when Dr. Rivera has to simply say no and he reminds himself and gives his assistants permission to say no when home time is more important. He understands that he could easily be a statistic if the work in the school becomes more important than his own family.

Striving for a state of mind where his personal and professional life is not separated helps Dr. Woods-Tucker find balance when he sees no real happy medium when living in both worlds. Dr. Woods-Tucker elaborates on the balance of work and family.

> I do not strive to create a happy medium between both worlds. Rather, I strive for a state of mind where I do not have to separate the two worlds. The stark reality is that too much time at work and you forsake the ones you love; too much time at home and with the children and you forsake your livelihood.
>
> I will never forget the following words that John Bandow, my former colleague in the Hilliard City, Ohio School District, shared with me 20 years ago, "This job provides a paycheck, but never sacrifice your family, your calling to serve, or your integrity."
>
> In my pursuit to make time for both worlds, we have committed as a family to ensuring (1) Sunday night is family night at the Tucker's household in which we eat dinner at 5 p.m. and watch a movie; (2) each summer we vacation for a week in Orlando, Florida; (3) every Labor Day we travel to Arkansas to spend the holiday in my hometown with nearly 100 of our relatives; and (4), most importantly, we serve the Lord in church by using our gifts to make an impact for Christ.

Dr. Woods-Tucker sees balance in his life when he can maintain his ability to serve his school and family while maintaining the highest level of integrity. He ensures that he dedicates time with his family during the week, through vacations and service to his faith.

Takeaways

- Superintendents struggle to maintain balance as they seek personal solutions.
- Superintendents experience tension between finding time for their work and family but family needs must come first.
- Superintendents cannot share the space at work and home at the same time—you are either with your family or doing your work but cannot do both very well at the same time.

Reflecting on the Work

Your balance is the system's balance . . .

1. In what ways are you able to make time for both work and family?

SLEEPING AT NIGHT

The work life for superintendents can easily take its toll as they assume the responsibility to educate all children. Staying awake or waking up at night thinking about the work is a staple for superintendents. Behind the sleeplessness or waking up in the middle of the night and not getting back to sleep is often a result of the mental strain and endless ruminations caused by the complexities of the decisions made every day.

A problem that keeps you up at night may not actually be a problem at all according to Mr. Dennis Dearden. He has learned to not stay awake for most problems because they just did not materialize. Mr. Dearden gives perspective about the workday strain that trails through the night from the weight of the job responsibilities.

> Turning work off when you get home and turning your attention to your loved ones and being in the moment with them is the first step. I learned very early as superintendent that 90 percent of all the things that I was worrying about never happened or were taken care of successfully by the staff members that I assigned the task to. It was a matter of trusting the staff to do the job I hired them to do. I had to come to grips that to be successful, I did not personally have to do everything.
>
> Having great people around you, a solid plan, and continually building trust are most important. Remember, that trust always goes back to zero when leadership changes. It takes time to build trust with your staff and community. Once

the trust exists it will go a long way to making you have a great night's sleep. It is worth the effort.

Working with a talented staff helps minimize the strain of the superintendent because they know it will be handled correctly. With a talented team, a high level of trust can be developed which leads to good decisions and affords a restful night's sleep for the superintendent.

Professional peace of mind provides Dr. Thomas Woods-Tucker with the confidence required in making the right decisions to move forward. He understands the need for self-renewal every night. Dr. Woods-Tucker provides perspective about the workday strain that trails through the night from the weight of the job responsibilities.

> My professional peace of mind comes from going to work each day, giving my "all" to my students and staff, knowing I've done right by them. Everything else will come. My spiritual peace of mind comes from regular time in prayer and meditation that prepare me for a good night's rest and renewal.
>
> Proverbs 3:5–6 says: "Trust in the LORD with all your heart; and lean not on your own understanding. In all your ways acknowledge him, and he shall direct your paths." Learning how to meditate or "still myself in prayer" has helped me improve my focus and lower my overall stress levels. Prayer and meditation have forced me to live in the present. When we "still ourselves," we are able to listen and find the peace to sleep well at night.

Meditation and prayer keep Dr. Woods-Tucker in the present and through faith, he does not rely only on himself to find direction. By stilling himself in prayer, he is able to lower stress levels that lead him to the peace needed to sleep at night.

Dr. Rivera finds he can physically sleep at night due to the exhausting work and long hours every day. With that said, the physical nature of the work only accounts for the sleep when he has a clear conscience about staying true to his leadership values. Dr. Rivera provides perspective about the workday strain that trails through the night from the weight of the job responsibilities.

> I actually sleep very well at night; I just don't get enough of it. The pattern of late nights and early mornings means that I'm so tired that I fall asleep within minutes of my head hitting the pillow. However, my clear conscience at night doesn't come from going to bed fatigued; it's really about going to bed knowing that I stayed true to my leadership values.
>
> I believe we make decisions based on three priorities: children, programs, and staff. In that order, always and forever. I juggle sensitive issues and complex decisions during most days; almost everything can be simplified by applying that three-part filter. Such prioritization allows me to stay true to my leadership values and, equally as important, sleep well at night.

Dr. Rivera has a clear conscience needed for him to sleep at night when he prioritizes decisions. Expanding on this idea, Dr. Rivera's conscience becomes clear when he makes decisions about children first, programs second, and staff third.

Dr. Patrice Pujol often stays awake thinking about new ideas or possible solutions to problems. Dr. Pujol's method for dealing with issues that creep into her sleep space is to commit her ideas to writing so she can move on to sleep. Dr. Pujol provides perspective about the workday strain that trails through the night from the weight of the job responsibilities.

> I am a pretty light sleeper and it is not unusual for the inability to turn my brain off to keep me up at night. Over the years, I have found a few tricks to help me. One is I keep a notebook and my phone on my bedside table. If I wake up and think of something I have to do the following day, I immediately add it to my task list on my phone. If I am thinking through a project or next steps on something that is ongoing and I come up with an idea, I jot a few notes on my notepad. For some people these actions may be more sleep disruptive, but for me I am able to check them off until the morning allowing me to go back to sleep.
>
> I think the thing that can really keep you up at night is trying to puzzle through a decision, perhaps one to which there is no really good answer. Every superintendent has to have a process through which he or she gathers as much information as possible, confers with the appropriate people, analyzes pros and cons, determines risks and benefits, and then makes a decision. The key to being able to sleep at night is being at peace with your decision making process and with the knowledge that you have made the best decision you can make based on the information you have.
>
> That is all anyone can be asked to do. I have found that when a decision is weighing on me, I try not to procrastinate. I indeed perform due diligence and do the necessary fact finding, but I go ahead and make a decision and then live with it. When I am in the thralls of the turmoil and crisis that often surrounds the toughest decisions, I often think of one of my mother's favorite pieces of advice, "This too shall pass."
>
> No matter how difficult things may seem in the moment, life is transitory and the news cycle is short. Sometimes you just have to make the best decisions you know how to make and endure the heat until the next newsworthy thing comes along. At the end of the day, I try to put it all in perspective and know that even in the darkest times, there is goodness ahead and perhaps if I sleep on it, I will find a better path tomorrow.

When difficult decisions are made that keep a superintendent up at night, Dr. Pujol reminds us that soon another crisis will likely take its place. Even when she find herself at a difficult place, she acknowledges that there are always good things to come and this allows her to find sleep at night.

Takeaways

- Superintendents need to find an inner peace with how they make decisions.
- Superintendents do not carry it all on their shoulders when they have talented teams to make good decision along the way.
- Superintendents make many difficult decisions; therefore, do not stay awake for one as another will be right behind it.

Reflecting on the Work

Your balance is the system's balance . . .

1. How do you manage the work and pressures so you can garner peace of mind and a way to sleep at night?

SUMMARY

Creating a balance between beliefs, work responsibilities, family, and oneself is paramount to the health of a superintendent. It is as simple as this: a healthy superintendent equals a healthy school district. Balance is only achieved when one purposefully works toward this goal.

As evidenced by our colleagues, each one has an internal system that drives them to do what they do every day—sometimes to the brink of personal strain. However, each found a way to move forward to achieve what needed to be done to educate all children. The paths for keeping healthy are many but the result is one—all children.

In chapter 9, the central themes across all the chapters are offered as a way to recap the most salient ideas from this book. Moreover, key elements of the book come together to create a holistic picture of the emerging role of the superintendent as they shift their focus to change the lives of all children.

A SUPERINTENDENT'S DIVE INTO PERSONAL
AND PROFESSIONAL BALANCE

1. Write a letter to a parent, relative, or friend and let them know how your childhood life and school experiences drives your work every day.
2. Completely separate your work time from time with your family (include phones computers, iPads, etc.) for two weeks. Then reflect on how it helped in balancing your work and personal life.
3. Ask your family members to give you one change you could make in your work life to help them in their life—and then do it!

SUGGESTED READINGS

Carlson, R., and Bailey, J. (2009). *Slowing down to the speed of life*. New York, NY: HarperCollins Publishers.

Katherine, A. (2012). *Where to draw the line: How to set healthy boundaries every day*. New York, NY: Simon & Schuster.

Kelly, M. (2011). *Off balance: Getting beyond the work-life balance myth to personal and professional satisfaction*. New York, NY: Penguin Random House, LLC.

Taylor, T. A. (2013). *The balance myth: Rethinking work-life success*. Austin, TX: Greenleaf Book Group.

Chapter 9

We Are All Responsible

IN THIS CHAPTER . . .

- Engage in New Thinking by Asking Different Questions
- Ensure the Work of the District Impacts Every Student
- Redefine the Roles and Relationships of Adults
- Develop and Support Transformational Leadership
- Understand Your Journey
- Lead for Coherence

INTRODUCTION

The emerging role of superintendents in transforming schools creates new and significant opportunities that can improve the learning experiences for all children. The nature of this work is complex, it is personal, and it evokes philosophical perspectives not only for the superintendent but also for the members of the community, including leaders in the business, faith-based, health, and governmental sectors that have responsibilities for developing youth. Ultimately, the superintendent holds the responsibility to create an environment to ensure all students receive an education that prepares them for their futures.

The message for superintendents is that the work ahead will not be easy because change requires everyone to have agreements on how to get the desired results. We hope you were able to use the content and reflections to understand better who you are as the leader in your school district and community. In this chapter, we offer six themes that were common throughout each of the eight preceding chapters.

To focus reflection on the big messages of the book, we posed overarching questions within each section of this chapter. Questions are important because they lead people to think and to imagine what is possible. We remind the reader that this book is not a how-to book. Its primary purpose is to help leaders think about leading new systems to engage the internal and external stakeholders who work on behalf of students and their families. There is a sense of urgency to lead on a foundation that educating all students is an adult responsibility and not a student problem.

ENGAGE IN NEW THINKING BY ASKING DIFFERENT QUESTIONS

To engage in leading the transformation of schools, superintendents need to ask of themselves tough questions, including, for example: are they ready to ask different questions to ensure that every student can access their education? In addition, are they willing to make the changes necessary for this to occur? Change can only be initiated when the adults create a clear direction that includes initiatives that benefit every student. Adults have a responsibility to create a common language around educational practices that can be understood and implemented with fidelity.

In transforming schools, processes for monitoring and making midcourse changes around innovative initiatives starts with the school board and superintendent and includes every member of the school community. To keep efforts on track, critical questions for every leader to ask are: "Are we doing what we said we would do?" and, "How is the work aligned to our vision, mission, and beliefs?"

The world around us is not like the one in which most of us were educated. This discrepancy raises many questions across many areas. No two areas are more important than asking about the shifts in communities and the mandate to rethink the skills students will need to be successful in their future. The success of students is influenced by what they experience both inside and outside of the school. Now, the superintendent must take the lead in rethinking an often narrow focus on schools having the primary responsibility for educating students.

To broaden this view, superintendents must consider the totality of student needs. New questions and their answers will necessitate creating a different learner profile. This new learner profile can be leveraged to provide leaders with new opportunities to build newer and more responsive systems, if they are willing to take risks on behalf of children. We must ask ourselves, "Are the current systems more about what adults want rather than what students need?" and then ask, "What future will our students have once they leave the system and walk into their futures?"

Superintendents do not need to prove their authority; instead, they must demonstrate that they are teachers of leaders. Leadership in every corner of the district and in their communities requires the confidence of the superintendent to empower others to make new and different decisions. Those within the system have the greatest opportunity to generate innovative ideas to create new opportunities. Empowering others and modeling leader qualities develops a new culture of change through innovation and risk-taking.

We believe that making significant shifts in transforming schools can only be sustained when superintendents lead leaders into a voice of one. The voice of one is developed through many processes but none is more important than that of effective governance. Self-reflective questions for superintendents and school board members keeps the focus on effective governance defined by roles and responsibilities. Governance in support of the district's direction is either positively or negatively influenced by how adults model approaching their responsibilities. Governance is very public, and social media brings an immediacy to the impact of board behaviors as they make decisions.

ENSURE THE WORK OF THE DISTRICT IMPACTS EVERY STUDENT

When leaders espouse their beliefs about educating all children, many questions emerge including for example, 1) Is this the right work? and 2) Is the work across the system affecting all children? In many systems, the work is defined in the strategic plan but is diluted to the point where there is very little impact from the lack of shared and clearly understood expectations. To affect all students requires coherence in the systems. Monitoring systems to assess both implementation and effectiveness ensure alignment. Superintendents must have confidence that the work of the district has the fullest impact on all students to ensure that students in the system are no longer marginalized.

We know that community organizations and schools often work in silos. As our communities change and students with their families are challenged in meeting their social, emotional, and physical needs, new collaborative partnerships need to be developed. Students and their families can only get the support they need when schools and community organizations recognize how their collective assets help all and not just some.

Schools and external organizations will need to align their philosophies and actions so that their decisions support new processes with new outcomes. Meeting the needs of all children will require risks when moving away from the "norm." Stepping more into the unknown landscape of educating students in a world of access requires leaders to have conviction about how the changing technology space can bring equal access to education. The access gap, which continues to grow, will only continue to widen if leaders choose to let it do so. Closing the access gap to where all students have web access is paramount to changing instructional delivery systems, so all students acquire the new skills they need.

Assessing the district impact on every student goes well beyond test scores and many of the current evaluative metrics used at state and federal levels. Superintendents stand at a pivotal point where their voices can change the course of education. The responsibility to impact decisions at the state and federal levels cannot be relegated to any degree of passivity. Developing strong relations with decision-makers and leveraging a strong voice in advocating for schools and new instructional delivery systems is no longer an option.

The fast-growing infusion and accessibility of social media has great potential in aligning and communicating the work of school districts. Establishing a brand provides the internal and external stakeholders with a direction for the district and with the vision and mission, creating unity. Social media systems can help leaders get valuable information from stakeholders in developing, monitoring, and assessing new initiatives. Creating and maintaining a culture where those in the system are engaged in the change process is instrumental in giving change input to help align, validate, and sustain the work.

REDEFINE THE ROLES AND RELATIONSHIPS OF ADULTS

When leaders and members of governing boards talk about change in schools, two questions come to mind: 1) Are they willing to reflect on their own ability to change and think differently? and 2) Are they willing to assume new roles in the processes needed to enact change? In too many instances, districts and their communities have been caught up in the interpersonal catastrophes as the adults speak about change and take positions about how to educate children.

Often, disagreements get personal and distract from the real work—educating all children. The days of "ugly" discourse and pointing the finger of blame to others and their organizations must stop, quickly. Children can no longer be the recipients of adult blame. Blame does not fix, nor does it reflect the collaborative qualities we ask students to seek in themselves. Adults have ideologies but need to be prepared to take risks with their own thinking rather than convincing others to change theirs.

The relationships of the adults in schools and in the community need to be redefined to establish collective efforts to support the varied needs of children as communities change. No longer are the boundaries of schools so finite as to limit the scope of responsibilities that each adult assumes. Schools cannot do it alone. Schools and communities must collaborate in a unified manner to assume roles to support children.

The work of leading adults to unify around the needs of children is challenging but critical as superintendents recommend and navigate significant changes within their systems. It is here where the roles of those in decision-making positions of governance need to balance the pressures to work with multiple belief systems and the negative noise while making difficult decisions. Clarity in the roles and responsibilities remain central to effective governance and often requires in-depth examination by the superintendent and others to move the district forward with an "educate all children" agenda.

Everyone wants their ideas to be heard and understood. For superintendents, reconciling the many voices and roles of the adults in and out of the system is monumental and often appears as an impossible undertaking. The use of social media has broad implications on the leader's ability to engage adults to see the value of their roles in the organizations and to create a greater sense of commitment to the work. Social media allows new voices to be heard and new ideas introduced in ways for adults to understand and affirm their responsibilities and expand their roles in the systems. The adults will be more readily willing to understand their roles in systems when given a voice along with the voice of others.

DEVELOP AND SUPPORT
TRANSFORMATIONAL LEADERSHIP

When superintendents talk about leadership and the expectations of leaders in the systems, do they expect them 1) to lead schools for the future? and 2) to support and develop leadership in their divisions or schools? New ideas cannot be developed or sustained if leaders do not believe in and support the change. Leaders ready to forward the work of schools need to have the autonomy to champion initiatives in their schools. However, autonomy is not an exemption from the direction and beliefs of the organization. To the contrary, transformation practices originating at all levels of the system support what the district describes for their children.

Transformational leaders cannot delegate their role as instructional leaders. For this reason alone, leaders need to understand how instructional design supports the knowledge and skills students will need because their future will not look like anything in our lives today. The digital landscape has changed the access for learning, necessitating a shift away from traditional deliveries presently in schools.

If superintendents see themselves as transformational leaders, then supporting other leaders in the system requires opportunities for them to gain new insights as changes are introduced, implemented, and assessed. Modeling the qualities of effective leadership requires great patience but potentially has the most significant impact on the system. The adults are in the public eye of students and what they see in adults taking responsibility is how they see leadership within themselves.

People in formal leader positions can no longer be the only ones to hold leadership roles. The ability to lead emerges when people are empowered to engage and grow in a leadership capacity. Leaders develop when superintendents build a culture that has the capacity to recognize and develop people across all parts of the system. A culture of leader growth and development emerges when superintendents move from the statement "Do what I ask" to the question of "What is your thinking?"

UNDERSTAND YOUR JOURNEY

To reflect on their journey about becoming superintendents, there is really only one critical question: "How do I dedicate all of my energy and thought to leading schools while giving the same amount and more energy to my personal and family life?" This question is one that has no patent answer, if one at all. No different from the stress in any job, superintendents need to stay healthy if their systems are going to be healthy.

While prioritizing helps to organize a superintendent's work load, the reality is that often they have little opportunity to say, "I can do this next week" because there is an inherent urgency for all the work that must be accomplished. Health and balancing one's personal life is equally as important, and in some instances, perhaps more important. A tension is found in the phrase, "take care of your family" because the stark reality is that the work of the superintendent and those in the system become extended family. Finding work and life balance is a journey every day.

The emerging requirement for superintendents is to lead their school districts in meeting the needs of diverse populations. This work has become a Herculean task. The responsibilities of superintendents require them to have strong skills in managing millions of dollars in budgets, leading thousands of employees, designing and building new schools for the future, and being a teacher to thousands of students. Now add to this professional list—a community leader, teacher of leaders, design technology expert, political lobbyist, and social worker, with the full responsibility for the safety, growth, and development of over 50 million students in this country. Leading schools in this country is not a "day job" but an all day, all night, on weekends and holiday job, and more.

The pressures to bear on improving not only the learning outcomes of children but also the learning conditions for children to succeed is unprecedented. Superintendents now need to reach beyond the schoolhouse steps to lead by asking new questions such as:

1. How can I be the instructional leader of the district while understanding how to best leverage resources to meet the overall needs of *all* children that improve their ability to learn?
2. How do I know the right questions to ask when seeking solutions to new problems not previously encountered, and how do I respond to questions when the outcomes are unclear?
3. How do I create new instructional designs that are untested, knowing that we must take these risks if children are going to succeed?

These are just the "tip of the iceberg" questions that superintendents will be asking themselves every day.

LEAD FOR COHERENCE

When superintendents create turbulence through transformation, critical questions help keep the system balanced. Two such questions include: 1) How does a superintendent lead from the vision, mission, and beliefs to ensure coherence during the turbulence of change? and 2) What processes are necessary to create coherence amid the moving parts that emerge as programs evolve based on the constantly changing needs of children, their families, and the changing communities in which they reside?

Coherence is built around the language superintendents use to frame and describe the work and conversations. Questions to ask might include:

1. Do we all speak and take action around a common language?
2. Do I communicate the same message or brand about the work and its value to children?
3. Do the conversations I have with teachers, site-level leaders, the board of education, community members, and other constituents communicate the same message?

Through directed questioning, superintendents can determine if, where, and how systems are aligned. To achieve coherence, information must flow throughout the system to ensure that the intentionality of actions result in the connections and relationships among the parts. Leaders bring coherence to this work through direction and creating the synergy for their actions to move the system. Changes in the system are sustained and become part of the culture when leaders understand how the power of unity can bring coherence across many moving parts.

As districts become adept at making changes, ensuring system coherence becomes the centering element that keeps the system from becoming a collection of random actions. Superintendents can navigate and sustain systems by putting in place processes to ensure policies, allocation of resources, use of human resources, and community voices move the system together as one. Coherence for school systems minimizes the distractions while maximizing and sustaining the actions needed to carry forward the system mission, vision, and beliefs to fruition.

SUMMARY

Education is the foundation of this country. One sixth of our nation's population, over 50 million students, walk through the doors of schools across this country every day. We wrote this book for superintendents and school leaders because there is no greater importance or urgency than to ensure that all students grow in every aspect of their lives. Leading education for tomorrow and not today requires new questions to be asked with courage, tenacity, and conviction.

SUGGESTED READINGS

Blank, M. J., Jacobson, R., & Melaville, A. (2012). *Achieving results through community school partnerships: How district and community leaders are building effective, sustainable relationships*. Washington, DC: The Center for American Progress.

Bryk, A. S., Gomez, L. M., Grunow, A., & LeMahieu, P. G. (2015). *Learning to improve: How America's schools can get better at getting better*. Cambridge, MA: Harvard Education Press.

Garvey Berger, J., & Johnston, K. (2015). *Simple habits for complex times: Powerful practices for leaders*. Stanford, CA: Stanford University Press.

Hirsh, S., & Foster, A. (2013). *A school board guide to leading successful schools: Focusing on learning*. Thousand Oaks, CA: Corwin Press.

Lubelfeld, M., & Polyak, N. (2017). *The unlearning leader: Leading for tomorrow's schools today*. Lanham, MD: Rowman & Littlefield.

Magette, K. (2014). *Embracing social media: A practical guide to manage risk and leverage opportunity*. Lanham, MD: Rowman & Littlefield.

Purinton, T., & Azcoitia, C. (Eds.). (2016). *Creating engagement between schools and their communities: Lessons from educational leaders*. Lanham, MD: Rowman & Littlefield.

Reimer, L. E. (2015). *Leadership and school boards: Guarding the trust in an era of community engagement* (2nd ed.). Lanham, MD: Rowman & Littlefield.

Supovitz, J. A., & Spillane, J. P. (2015). *Challenging standards: Navigating conflict and building capacity in the era of the Common Core*. Lanham, MD: Rowman & Littlefield.

Thomas, D., & Brown, J. S. (2011). A new culture of learning: Cultivating the imagination for a world of constant change. Lexington, KY: CreateSpace.

Tschannen-Moran, M., & Tschannen-Moran, B. (2017). *Evoking greatness: Coaching to bring out the best in educational leaders*. Thousand Oaks, CA: Corwin Press.

White, P. C., Harvey, T. R., & Fox, S. L. (2016). *The politically intelligent leader: Dealing with the dilemmas of a high-stakes educational environment* (2nd ed.). Lanham, MD: Rowman & Littlefield.

Wilhoit, G., Pittenger, L., & Rickabaugh, J. (2016). *Leadership for Learning: What is leadership's role in supporting success for every student?* Lexington, KY: Center for Innovation in Education.

Index

About the Authors

Philip D. Lanoue, PhD, is one of the leading voices in educational leadership and transformation. He has a demonstrated record in leading at the building and district levels. Dr. Lanoue is the 2015 American Association of School Administrators (AASA) National Superintendent of the Year, as well as the 2015 Georgia Superintendent of the Year. Before serving at the superintendent level across two systems in Georgia, Dr. Lanoue was a high school principal in Vermont and Massachusetts, leading four schools toward excellence. His work appears in a variety of publications, including refereed journal articles and invited chapters in edited books.

Sally J. Zepeda, PhD, is professor at the University of Georgia in the Department of Lifelong Education, Administration, and Policy. She teaches courses related to instructional supervision and theory, teacher evaluation, and professional development. Dr. Zepeda's research focuses on these areas and the work of school principals and superintendents related to succession and leadership development. Dr. Zepeda has written 32 books and countless articles and book chapters, and she continues to work extensively with school districts in the United States and internationally.